The Tyranny of Big Tech

THE TYRANNY OF BIG TECH

JOSH HAWLEY

Regnery

1947 | **75** YEARS | 2022
WASHINGTON, D.C.

Regnery® is a registered trademark and its colophon is a trademark of Salem Communications Holding Corporation

Cataloging-in-Publication data on file with the Library of Congress

First trade paperback edition published 2022

ISBN: 978-1-68451-337-6
Library of Congress Control Number: 2021304054

Published in the United States by
Regnery Publishing
A Division of Salem Media Group
Washington, D.C.
www.Regnery.com

Manufactured in the United States of America

10 9 8 7 6 5 4 3 2 1

Books are available in quantity for promotional or premium use. For information on discounts and terms, please visit our website: www.Regnery.com.

To Erin

CONTENTS

PREFACE

This is a book the corporate monopolies did not want you to read. Corporate America tried to cancel it, just as they have tried to cancel me and to cancel or control the speech, the communication, even the ideas of millions of Americans—*all* Americans, in a sense, because what the woke capitalists want, along with their allies in government, is to preserve their power over American politics and society. They have been working to entrench that power for the better part of a century, since the age of the last robber barons, and they are not about to see it challenged now. This book presents a challenge nevertheless: it calls into question the reigning order of corporate liberalism, and it challenges the power of those who benefit from it. And I hope that after reading it, you will want to challenge the corporate liberal order too. I hope you will want to work to revive what is properly the birthright of all Americans, the republic of the common man and woman.

It will take some doing. The framers of our Constitution feared aristocracy—"faction," James Madison called it, rule by the enterprising few. But that is in fact what we have in America today. The titans of woke capital, and of Big Tech above all, lead the most powerful corporations in history. They have amassed that power with the active aid of government, and now together Big Tech and Big Government seek to extend their influence over every area of American life.

If you doubt this, look only at the furious assault on free speech by Big Tech and its fellow corporatists in the early days of 2021. Following the grisly riot at the U.S. Capitol on January 6, Big Tech quickly moved to silence conservative voices. The major tech companies de-platformed a bevy of conservatives, including the president of the United States. In a matter of days, Big Tech brought down the independent social media platform Parler: Apple and Google refused to make Parler available in their app stores, and Amazon soon denied Parler access to its cloud computing service. Other major corporations got in on the act. Banks reportedly turned over private information about their customers if they had been in or around Washington, D.C., on January 6.

One of the largest publishers in the nation cancelled this book, citing my "role" in the events of January 6. My sin? Not encouraging the riot, as the publisher certainly knew. I fiercely condemned the violence and the thugs who perpetrated it, just as I had condemned all civil violence and rioting during the months of unrest that unfolded across the country in 2020. No, my sin was to raise an objection to one state during the electoral college certification process, thereby triggering a congressional debate, precisely as permitted by the law and precisely as Democratic members of Congress have done in the electoral counts of 2001, 2005, and 2017. I was, in fact, waiting to participate in that debate on the Senate floor when the riot halted our work and forced the Senate (temporarily) to disband. For this I was branded a "seditionist" and worse. But like many others attacked by the corporations and the Left, my real crime was to have challenged the reign of the woke capitalists.

Since I arrived in the Senate in early 2019, I have relentlessly targeted the power and pretensions of the Big Tech monopolies. The weeks following January 6 demonstrated their frightening, tremendous reach: power over information, over news, over communication and social debate. Even Angela Merkel expressed disquiet at Big Tech's censorial campaign. But none of this was new. Tech had been amassing power for some time, gathering influence at every opportunity, more with every passing year, and all with the helping hand of government. It was government that fueled the tech oligarchs' rise with special protections in federal law. It was elected politicians who cheered on Big Tech's censorship—and called for more—in the closing years of the 2010s and the opening days of 2021.

Big Tech wants to transform America, that's clear; it wants to remake our society in its image. But in this regard, Big Tech is no different from the earlier oligarchs who made its rise possible. Up until a century ago, most Americans regarded monopoly and corporate concentration with profound distrust. The founders associated it with aristocracy, and they believed aristocracy was a death sentence for republics. Accordingly, they strictly limited corporate power, banned monopolies in all but the rarest cases, and worked to establish an economy of independent producers— where the common person, the common laborer, would have political influence and sway. In fact, earlier Americans believed the republic depended on the strength of the working man and woman. These were the most virtuous of citizens, Thomas Jefferson said. The early Americans celebrated labor and the dignity of ordinary life—hearth and home, work and family. They believed the republic was meant to protect that life and the people who lived it. And for that, the common person needed to have a share in self-government. That's what liberty was.

That changed—or began to—a century ago, when a group of corporate barons argued that monopoly wasn't such a bad thing after all. They contended that economic concentration was inevitable, even necessary, for progress. They characterized the economy of independent producers the founding generation had known and labored to uphold as outmoded. They advocated instead a new hierarchy in America, with the capitalists and their professional manager class at the top and mere labor down below. As for liberty, they argued it had little to do with the common man's share in self-government. Liberty was the private space government and the professional class agreed to leave you in the country they now ran.

The corporate barons of the Gilded Age succeeded in bringing their vision, their corporate liberalism, to America. Big Tech is their natural successor. Like the barons of the Gilded Age, today's tech oligarchs wield immense power, thanks to a combination of government aid and monopoly; like the barons, they are utterly convinced of their own righteousness and their right to govern America. Our republic has never been more hierarchical, more riven by class, more managed by an elite than it is today. That is corporate liberalism's legacy. But it need not be our future.

This book is an exercise in alternative possibilities, an attempt to recover a different way of thinking about society and politics; it is an attempt, most fundamentally, to recover the meaning of the common man's republic. It is not too late to make it real again.

PART I

CHAPTER 1

THE RETURN OF THE MONOPOLIES

Back in September of 2019, Mark Zuckerberg paid me a visit. He delivered himself to my door on Capitol Hill with a retinue of lobbyists and "governmental affairs" people in train, cameras whirring, reporters shouting, the whole Big Tech baronial circus right there on the second floor of the Russell Senate Office Building. Zuckerberg wanted to talk about Facebook, of course, his gift to the world, and why, on his telling, that mighty tech behemoth was utterly deserving of all the special giveaways and protections it enjoyed from the United States government.

We met in a narrow room across a long, varnished table, he on one side, I on the other, with a handful of staff flanking each of us. Light poured in from a high Norman window. We were arrayed as if negotiating the conclusion of some global conflagration, though this meeting brought no end of hostilities. On the contrary. Zuckerberg had asked to meet approximately two months earlier. By then I had been in the Senate only a matter of months—I was its youngest member—and I had devoted much of that early time to the problem of Big Tech. Within weeks of taking my oath, I proposed new protections for children online and new rights for parents to guard their family's privacy.[1] I proposed limits to tech's addictive design features and reforms to confront tech's political censorship.[2] This followed from my efforts as Missouri attorney general to investigate Facebook (and Google) for antitrust and consumer protection violations.[3] I was the first state attorney general in the nation to launch such a probe. Facebook, Inc. was not amused.

Zuckerberg originally proposed we meet in California, at his headquarters in Silicon Valley. I refused. The point of a meeting like this was to *make* a point, to put down a marker. My aim was to confront him on the real issue at stake, the power of his monopoly, to force that question to the fore. I was not about to travel to Facebook central command to be part of some corporate photo op. I suggested we meet in Missouri, my home. We finally compromised on my Senate office in Washington. By the time Zuckerberg arrived at my doorstep that afternoon in September, he had been in the capital for a day or more, making the rounds, hosting exclusive dinners—I was always amazed at the number of senators and congressmen who fawned over his invitations—applying a personal touch. Our meeting in my office came toward the end of his charm offensive.

He arrived prepared to reason with me, I could see. His demeanor was polite. His tone was patient, explanatory. He was even ready to make concessions. He acknowledged Facebook had wrongly de-platformed a pro-life group, Live Action—"We made a mistake," he said—and suggested that the problem might be systemic. "We have a bias problem at Facebook," he said. He promised action to address political bias. He also nodded to the problem of privacy, said he wanted to protect kids online, and pledged new steps to address the growing issue of online addiction. His agenda, in short, was to make Facebook a model corporate citizen. And all he needed the Senate to do was . . . nothing. Stay out of it. Let Facebook right its ship. Or if the Senate were inclined to do something, then impose privacy regulations of the kind Facebook was already complying with, conveniently, and be sure to apply them to *smaller* companies as well, start-ups and so forth, lest competition get out of hand.

Which was about the time I decided to get to the heart of the matter. You talk about competition and privacy and ending unfair censorship, I said. But it's your monopoly that gives you the power to do all those things. So let's get serious. Stop buying off competitors. Stop throttling competition. *Prove* you're ready to change. End your monopoly: sell Instagram and WhatsApp. Break up the Facebook empire.

Zuckerberg sat silent for a moment following this challenge, blinking. His government-affairs people glowered from their chairs. I would not be getting invited to any of those glittering "private dinners with Mark," I could see. A moment later, Zuckerberg replied, his patient tone turned to outrage. "I don't even know what to say to this," he said. "That's absurd. That is not going to happen." Which, of course, was the whole point.

Facebook was not about to give up its monopoly. It was one of the most powerful companies in America since the heyday of the Gilded Age, a century before. It was not about to surrender power, not willingly. Facebook and its fellow Big Tech platforms—Google, Twitter, Amazon, and Apple—wanted to run the American economy, they wanted to run the *country*, and by that September in 2019, they were increasingly in position to do so. And all I could think, as I sat across that long table from Mark Zuckerberg, modern-day robber baron, was that America had again entered the age of the monopolists. They were back, as powerful and menacing to our republic as they had been a century before, as detrimental to the rule of decent, ordinary people as they had been when Theodore Roosevelt and his trust-busting compatriots famously confronted them. Now we needed Roosevelt's example again.

■ ■ ■

I had studied Theodore Roosevelt and written about him some years before. In my battle with the monopolists as attorney general and then in the Senate, I found myself again returning to him, our boldest of presidents, revisiting his policies, his speeches, his call to defend the republic. Yes, the republic. For Roosevelt, the American republic was not merely a form of government, but a way of liberty, a way of *life* premised on the dignity of the common man and dependent on the common person's strength and independence. Roosevelt believed that liberty had more to it than the right to be let alone. It was the right to have a say in one's nation, to help shape the future of the community one called home, to exercise the power and mastery of a citizen.

The problem was, Theodore Roosevelt had not succeeded all those years ago. His renown as a trust-buster notwithstanding, he never managed fully to banish the monopolists. Instead, it was the corporate barons who succeeded in imposing on the nation a complete reconstruction of the American economy, organized around the giant corporation. And they imposed along with it a complete reconstruction of American life. This first generation of corporate barons left a lasting, if dubious, legacy: they made America more hierarchical, with new divisions between management and labor, between a professional class and everyday workers. They made the economy more centralized, consolidating power into a few mega-companies and their owners; they made it more globalized, keyed to international capital and trade. They diminished the voice of the ordinary citizen in society and politics in favor of educated, professionalized elites. In short, they gave America an entirely new political economy, what some historians have called corporate liberalism.[4] A century later, we are still living with it, and with its implications.

The rise of the new monopolists is one of them. Big Tech represents today's robber barons, who are draining prosperity and power away from the great middle of our society and creating, as they do, a new oligarchy. They do it by siphoning off consumers' personal data, employing a vast network of digital surveillance that tracks everything from a person's website visits to his travel to the barometric pressure of his location. And they do it by gobbling up individuals' creative contributions and work product, relentlessly relabeling information as "public domain" so they can feed it into their vast data machines, run by super-secret codes called algorithms.

The effect is that Big Tech makes more and more money, while the working class narrows and declines, diminished by Big Tech's Big Data and the "free" services Big Tech uses to collect that data in the first place. But that's not all. Big Tech's business model is based principally on data collection and advertising, which means devising ways to manipulate individuals to change their behavior—and then selling that opportunity at manipulation to big corporations. The result? An addiction economy designed to keep us online as much as possible, as long as possible, to sell us more and more stuff and collect more and more information.

Meanwhile, Big Tech increasingly controls the channels of communication in this country, personal and political; it controls the delivery of the news; it controls the avenues of commerce.

Like the corporate barons of a century ago, the tech titans hold themselves out as pioneers of a new economy, in this case an information economy of increased flexibility and choice for workers—supposedly. It hasn't worked out that way. The Big Tech economy is one presided over by a few titans who use our own data and information to make fortunes while stifling competition and currying favor with government to protect themselves from challenge or change.

Consider the merest sampling of their power. Facebook: Of adults in America who use social media, 99 percent use Facebook.[5] That's nearly 70 percent of *all* adults in the country. And that's just the main Facebook platform. Facebook also owns Instagram, WhatsApp, and Facebook Messenger, creating a user base so big the company can and has single-handedly reshaped the flow of information in the United States. News operations now optimize their stories for distribution on Facebook and go out of business when they don't—or when Facebook, on a whim, changes its algorithm to deemphasize their content.[6] Politicians spend outrageous sums of money trying to find voters there, more than on television or radio or any other platform.

Google is equally, if not more, powerful. Nine out of every ten searches on the internet in America are performed by Google Search, and when you consider how many Americans now use Google to get their basic information on everything from weather to sports to current events, Google's ability to direct the content we consume is unprecedented.[7] Google's browser, Chrome, holds 68 percent of the global desktop market share and 63 percent of the market for mobile browsing.[8] Its phone, Android, represents 85 percent of smartphone market share worldwide.[9] Even Google Maps is huge, controlling 67 percent of the smartphone map market.[10] More than any other company, Google knows exactly where you are, what you are doing, and with whom. And more than any other entity, it has the ability to shape Americans' first impressions on any subject.

Twitter is a social media power in its own right, boasting hundreds of millions of users and a particular ability to shape breaking news and journalistic opinion.[11]

Then there's Amazon. By 2020, the company boasted 126 million subscribers to its Amazon Prime subscription service, amounting to more than one-third of the nation.[12] That same year Amazon also controlled at least 40 percent of all online sales in America, giving it power over retail and commerce undreamt of by other, earlier American sales giants, to say nothing of the local retail stores it was in the process of destroying.[13]

As for Apple, its iPhone empire and the Apple App Store attached to it gave that tech giant a share in approximately $500 billion in annual app commerce—along with the ability to influence the design, marketing, and operation of every app offered up for sale on an iPhone.[14]

And what were the tech giants doing with all that influence, all that power? Reducing Americans to supplicants in their own country. Tech robs citizens of personal privacy with relentless surveillance and behavioral manipulation. Tech takes citizens' control over their property, their personal data. Then there is tech's war on our social and mental health. An accumulating tranche of research shows that Americans, and especially teenagers, who spend more time online are less happy, less socially engaged, and more vulnerable to addiction and suicide than those who do not. Big Tech's addiction business model is poisoning Americans' emotional and psychological well-being.

The tech platforms are destroying Americans' control over their lives in other ways, by manipulating what news Americans can see and influencing the political decisions they make. By 2019, Facebook was boasting it could change election outcomes. Facebook's vice president of augmented and virtual reality, Andrew Bosworth—"Boz," they call him at headquarters—claimed Facebook effectively made Donald Trump president in 2016. "So was Facebook responsible for Donald Trump getting elected?" Boz asked his fellow Facebookers in a company-wide post in 2019. "I think the answer is yes." He worried aloud Trump could win again in 2020, and thanks, again, to Facebook. It is "tempting," he wrote, "to use the tools available to us to change the outcome."[15] That outcome being a democratic election. In the days leading up to the 2020 presidential vote, Facebook and Twitter seemed determined to try. Both platforms censored the distribution of a *New York Post* report detailing illicit foreign profits by Joe Biden's son, Hunter, and alleging Joe Biden's potential involvement. The platforms suppressed the story until after the election was over. The Facebook platform was like the Ring of Power from the Tolkien books, Andrew Bosworth had told his colleagues.[16] It could rule them all—or rule the voters, in this case.

Research backs him up. Psychologist Robert Epstein testified to Congress in June 2019 that, based on his analysis, "if these companies all support the same candidate—and that's likely, needless to say—they will be able to shift upwards of 15 million votes to that candidate with no one knowing and without leaving a paper trail."[17]

Given just how much power Big Tech has amassed, and the profits the companies turn from it, perhaps it is not surprising that tech is willing to do nearly anything to keep it. The Federal Trade Commission began investigating Facebook as early as 2011 over allegations that it took and then broadcast personal information customers had designated as "private," while telling its customers just the opposite.[18] Facebook eventually agreed to pay a hefty fine for these bad acts, only to find itself back on the firing line eight years later for violating the settlement terms and continuing to take its customers' personal, private data.

This time Facebook paid $5 billion for its misdeeds while still refusing to formally admit any wrongdoing.[19]

In 2019, meanwhile, prosecutors for the European Union (EU) slapped Google with an unprecedented, multibillion-dollar fine for ad-related antitrust violations: Google had demanded its ad-buying customers sign contracts pledging not to advertise with or through other search platforms for years, before introducing "relaxed" restrictions on publishers forcing them to offer Google prime screen real estate.[20] That fine followed two others, one in 2017 and another in 2018, alleging Google had used its search engine to steer consumers to its own shopping platform and then separately forced the makers of its Android phones to preinstall Google apps.[21] All this in an effort to forestall competition from rivals. Altogether, the EU demanded $9.3 billion in antitrust fines.[22] Antitrust prosecutors in Europe opened similar probes of Amazon.[23]

Plenty of evidence suggested the same thing was happening in the United States. That is why I launched that antitrust investigation of Google in 2017 as attorney general of Missouri, and a similar investigation of Facebook shortly thereafter. Back then, I couldn't persuade a single other state attorney general to join me in the fight against the monopolists. By 2019, all fifty states had signed on to an antitrust probe of Google, along with the United States Department of Justice, which finally brought a formal antitrust suit in the fall of 2020.[24]

Big Tech's power, its hold on information and news and commerce, its business model of addiction and manipulation, is a danger not just to the working-class economy. Not just to our culture. This is a danger to the republic. The dominance of Big Tech threatens self-government by the great American middle, by the common man and woman. These modern-day robber barons threaten to centralize power in the hands of a few, while undermining the independence, economic standing, and cultural influence of everyone else. They are the culmination of that corporate liberalism installed a century ago by the first corporate barons—rule by the elite.

■ ■ ■

In Theodore Roosevelt's day, a great many Americans resisted the ambitions of the corporate barons in the name of liberty. They remembered an older tradition associated with the American founders and ascendant in the first century of American life, a tradition that inspired political figures and public movements from Thomas Jefferson to the Populists. This tradition emphasized the power of the common man and woman and their stake in self-government. It was sometimes called republicanism, and the trust-busters of that earlier era invoked it to resist the corporate takeover.

The republican tradition feared corporate power, or at least corporate power on any large scale. It feared the consolidation of wealth and privilege into a few hands. Republicanism favored an economy of independent producers and advocated policies to sustain a broad laboring class as the dominant influence in the nation. Republicanism saw labor as both noble and ennobling. It proclaimed working people as the best of citizens. And this tradition insisted that liberty was directly connected to the common citizen's ability to participate in his government, to have a say in politics and society. That's what a republic was: self-government by the common man, in defense of the common, ordinary way of life.

The republican tradition is harder to recall in our day. In the century since Theodore Roosevelt, corporate liberalism has become the reigning public philosophy of both Left and Right, accepted by the establishment of both major parties. The triumph of corporate liberalism has made it more difficult to remember why concentrated power is bad, whether in government or in private corporations. The corporate liberal consensus has made it harder to see why liberty is threatened by the rise of the new monopolists and by the continued decline of an independent working class. It has made it harder to fight back.

All of which is why the fight against Big Tech, these new monopolists, must ultimately reckon with the legacy of the old ones, with corporate liberalism. It must be a fight to recover the better understanding of liberty and the common person on which our republic was founded.

That is what this book is about. In the pages that follow, I set out as clearly as I can the dangers that Big Tech poses to all of us: its model of addiction, its surveillance and data theft, its menace to our children and our children's psychological well-being, its censorship, and its predatory form of globalism. I argue that we must confront Big Tech and break up its power.

But more than that, I argue that we must succeed where an earlier generation of trust-busters failed. We must challenge the corporate reconstruction of American life. We must challenge corporate liberalism. The tech barons have risen to power on the back of an ideology that blesses bigness—and concentrated power—in the economy and government. This ideology severs the tie between liberty and the power of the people to share in self-government. In fact, the corporate liberal creed deprecates the power of the common person altogether and turns government's operations and society's power over to experts and the professional class of educated elites. It has now reigned for a century and more. The time has come to end its hegemony and to reclaim the promise of our republic.

To do that, we must appreciate how we got where we are. To confront Big Tech, we must understand the tech barons' antecedents and the remodeling of the American regime those earlier robber barons pursued. Only then will we truly be able to understand our present situation and see our way toward change. And so my story begins at the turn of the last century, with the ambitions of the first robber barons, and with Theodore Roosevelt's failed attempt to stop them. With any luck, his failure may yet turn out to be temporary. We may yet be able to defend the republic.

CHAPTER 2

THE ROBBER BARONS

February 19, 1902. New York City. He had heard it at dinner, in the middle of what had otherwise been a pleasant evening, with no advance warning whatsoever. By morning the news was everywhere, in every newspaper of repute, on the lips of every trader and broker on Wall Street—shattering news that sent the stock market plunging, stunning news that had the bankers reeling, wholly unexpected news that threatened the empire he had worked so assiduously to construct over three decades . . . and all delivered to the world inside a dry little statement from someone named Philander Knox, who was, apparently, attorney general of the United States.[1] It began: "Within a very short time a bill will be filed by the United States to test the legality of the merger of the Northern Pacific and Great Northern [railroad] systems through the instrumentality of the Northern Securities Company."[2]

John Pierpont Morgan Sr. knew precisely what this meant. He had understood from the second he read the statement over his evening meal. It meant the Department of Justice was going to sue him. It meant the government of the United States was going to challenge his monopoly.

At age sixty-four, standing over six feet in height, with a famous ful-some mustache and bulbous nose that grew red with anger, J. P. Morgan—"Pierpont" to those who knew him—was perhaps the country's most famous financier and industrialist. He was the architect of U.S. Steel, the mastermind of General Electric, the principal of the nation's most profit-able railroad lines, and chairman of the richest, most powerful banking house in America, maybe the world.[3] He was a modern-day aristocrat, more powerful than any senator, than practically any president, a Master of the Universe ruling from his perch atop the House of Morgan. And he was not, to say the least, accustomed to hearing the word "No."

He did not like hearing it from the federal government in this Febru-ary of 1902. It was an affront, an outrage. How *dare* they. Had he not been careful to maintain good terms with government officials and to distribute his largesse widely? Had he not funded the politicians' cam-paigns? Why, he had even once helped save the federal treasury from financial ruin (and yes, he turned a handsome profit in the process, but business was business, and what was wrong with that?). He was a gener-ous philanthropist, a patron of the arts and science. He was, all told, a model citizen, a leading citizen, a friend to mankind. Was this how he was now to be repaid?

Furious, Morgan dispatched a team of lawyers to Washington City, as the capital was then sometimes known, on the morning of February 20. A day later, he decided to go himself. Wretched weather slowed his travel, and by the time he arrived Friday evening, February 21, Wash-ington was choked with snow and slush. Shards of ice clogged the sewer openings and banked water in the streets to the depth of a foot or more. Overnight, the temperature fell and the sludge turned to ice. The sudden freeze snapped telegraph wires and pulled down phone lines, so that by the morning of February 22, Washington was a frozen-over island of winter cut off from the rest of the world.[4]

Undeterred, Morgan emerged from his accommodations, the gilded Arlington Hotel at I Street and Vermont, and set out the two blocks for the White House. It was a Saturday.[5] He didn't care. He was going to see the man he held responsible for this imposition—that obnoxious, ungrateful, accidental twenty-sixth president of the United States, Theodore Roosevelt.

■ ■ ■

The story of Big Tech begins in the Gilded Age, with a class of corporate titans who paved the way for our own. Robber barons, the press called them, a grim title that suggested simultaneous opulence and rapacity. The capitalists of the *fin de siècle* displayed both. Their aim was to amass titanic fortunes, indeed, but more than that: they strove to change America. Like their successors in technology a century later, they saw themselves as the pioneers of an altogether new republic, the vanguard of an advanced era of progress and modernity. And they succeeded, in this sense: They gave the nation a new style of economy, and a new ideology to go with it. And they bequeathed both things to their technologist successors in the form of corporate liberalism. Which is why the story of the Gilded Age is also the story of our time.

The turn of the twentieth century brought a maelstrom of change to America, every bit as fierce and sudden as the one that heralded the beginning of the twenty-first: a radically new and industrializing economy, the emptying out of the countryside in favor of factory work in cities, railroads and telegraph lines that corseted the continent in a web of steel and wire, soaring levels of immigration. And presiding over it all, driving the storm of transformation forward at an ever more furious pace, was a new class of industrialists.

They became household names in their time, Cornelius Vanderbilt, the first of the lot, and Jay Gould and John D. Rockefeller and E. H. Harriman and James J. Hill and, seminally, John Pierpont Morgan. They amassed wealth the likes of which had never before been seen in America, and with it power—raw, unadulterated power—over government, over industry, over the nation. They were a caste unto themselves, a faction, an aristocracy of money, exactly what the American founders had feared.

And the means the barons used to entrench their power was one the founders feared too, an instrument the barons would leave to their Big Tech successors: the corporate monopoly. The corporate form had been banned in the early republic, available only for select public purposes—public works projects, generally—and only then when granted directly by states. The founding generation associated corporations with monopolies, and both with aristocracy, a direct threat to the class of independent workers on which the republic depended. The nineteenth-century capitalists revived the corporation and struggled to bring the whole of the American economy under its control. Rather than a nation of independent producers, the barons wanted a corporatized economy, dominated by a few giant monopolies, and—here was the key point—a corporate class to govern it. For to change the nation's economy was to change its character. And that was their agenda. That sturdy American yeoman, the common man, was to be swept aside as the dominant force in American life and replaced by the enlightened, sophisticated, corporate aristocracy. America would become a corporate republic.[6]

Not all Americans found this vision so enchanting. The struggle between the corporatists and those who—like the western farmers and the Populists and Theodore Roosevelt—resisted in the name of an older ideal, in the name of the common man's republic, would become the story of that time.[7] And the outcome of their struggle would define the story of ours.

■ ■ ■

The robber barons amassed their fortunes in a variety of connections, including finance and manufacturing. The most successful of them, like Pierpont Morgan, had a hand in every major industry. But the industry that led the field, that fired the engines of industrial growth in America and forged the new industrial elite, was the railroad.

America's first attempt at overland infrastructure had been the canal, the darling of early American luminaries from George Washington to

John Adams. Canal building was costly, however, and irredeemably slow. And even when finally finished, the canals could only be utilized in relatively warm weather, that is, when the waterways were not frozen. In the late 1830s, railroad building began as an alternative with a few tentative lines in the northeast, and then fairly exploded. Railroad mania came to New England in the 1840s and rolled on into the South and West a decade later.[8] In the 10 years of the 1850s, workers laid more than 21,000 miles of track. After a brief pause during the crisis of civil war, the building surged again. By the early 1870s, the country boasted over 70,000 track miles in operation, with nearly 200,000 by 1900.[9]

The railroads were a wonder, marvelous gargantuan things—the country's first genuinely big business concerns. They operated on a vast, continental scale, and they transformed everything they touched. They stimulated industrialization.[10] In the words of historian Alfred Chandler, "They did so directly, by providing a new market for the iron industry. And they did so indirectly, [. . .] by lowering the cost of transportation and opening up new areas to high-volume overland movement." They also made "possible a continuous flow—winter and summer—of raw and semi-finished material to the factory."[11]

They revolutionized finance. "Wall Street was invented to build the railroads," social historian Jack Beatty writes, "the first business enterprises in America too big for individuals or local investors to finance on their own."[12] In the 1850s, only a handful of the nation's largest factories were capitalized above $1 million.[13] By contrast, in 1859, investment in railroads had soared to $1 billion; the major East–West rail lines were capitalized at between $17 and $35 million apiece.[14] Most of the capital for the textile factories and other existing enterprise came from the regions where they were located, from local banks and their investors in Philadelphia and Boston. As for the railroads, the scale of investment needed was so prodigious and insatiable that they almost single-handedly spawned a new creature of finance, the investment bank, based usually in New York and dedicated to recruiting capital from around the nation and Europe. The famed House of Morgan was one of these.[15]

Then there was the scale of the railroads' employment. Before the Civil War, the biggest employer in America was the southern plantation, if you can call an enterprise of forced labor an "employer," and slaves constituted the largest workforce. Yet only 2 plantations in the country worked more than 1,000 slaves within their borders, and only 9 worked more than 500.[16] The largest textile factories in New England meanwhile employed fewer than 500 souls and almost never ran expenditures higher than $300,000. But the railroads, well—by 1862, the Pennsylvania Railroad *alone* churned out $12.2 million in annual costs. Soon it employed some 50,000 men.[17]

The sheer size and scale of rail lines led to innovations in business structure. The earliest railroads looked little different in management style from a New England factory. A fifty-mile road "might employ fifty men under a single superintendent."[18] But all that changed when the roads grew to encompass thousands upon thousands of miles of track. To deal with this awesome expanse and the intricacy of coordinating multiple moving parts and schedules, railroad owners devised an elaborate and rigid hierarchy of upper, middle, and lower management, with line workers at the very bottom. In Chandler's words, "No other business enterprise . . . had ever required the coordination and control of so many different types of units carrying out so great a variety of tasks that demanded such close scheduling."[19] The modern organization chart was born, and with it the modern divisions between ownership, management, and labor.[20]

As the railroads boomed, so too did the fortunes of those who owned them. Cornelius Vanderbilt, who made the first of his many millions as a steamboat manufacturer, switched to railroads in the 1840s—and started making serious money. Upon his death in 1877, he was worth north of $100 million, more than $100 *billion* in today's dollars.[21] Others followed where he led, taking advantage of generous government subsidies, including long-term loans and land grants for rail lines, to ignite a building frenzy.[22] New lines would spring up and build out only to go belly-up, sometimes taking down entire financial institutions with them—and then go into receivership, and then to a new owner, and the cycle would begin all over again. It was a rich man's gold rush, the capitalist Klondike, and one after another man of means dove headlong into the railway craze. By the 1880s, with thousands of miles of rail crisscrossing the map, the railroad magnates—those who had made it, whose lines had survived—were the richest men in America.[23]

They didn't hesitate to deploy those riches to their personal and corporate advantage. The railroads developed with the helping hand of government, and the railroad barons had every intention of preserving that relationship, but with the barons in the pole position. Predictably, they cultivated elected officials and financed political campaigns—but that was the least of it. In the states where their presence was greatest, they used their economic heft to suborn and direct entire state legislatures. One Kansas politician remembered that in the early 1890s, "[t]hree great railway systems governed [the state]. This was a matter of common knowledge. . . ."[24] Explained another: "Republican legislatures of Kansas simply obeyed the orders of railroad companies."[25] "[N]o candidate could be selected for any office, from township trustee to governor, who was objectionable to the Santa Fe" railroad.[26] Kansas was by no means peculiar. In Texas, California, New York, and nearly every state in between, the railroads made their influence—their power—felt.

And that power was obeyed. One survey of editorials from eleven different business journals between the years 1877 and 1896 regarding corporate influence in politics found the corporations' authority widely, ruefully acknowledged. Said the *Railway Review* in 1884, "No legislative body would dare to inaugurate or carry out . . . any measure without first knowing the pleasure of the manufacturing and commercial interests." The same publication reported in 1890, "Business and politics are now inextricably mixed up."[27]

The railroads had become a power unto themselves, a permanent interest, a faction, and by the 1870s their grasp reached all the way to the United States Congress. In the fall of 1872, the New York *Sun* reported explosive allegations that the Union Pacific Railroad, the first transcontinental rail line in the nation, chartered by Congress in 1862 and funded, in substantial part, by taxpayer subsidies, had distributed financial shares to members of the federal government in exchange for favors. In a word, it had bribed them. The Union Pacific's largest construction company was a group called Crédit Mobilier, which, it turns out, had rather brazenly overcharged the railroad for much of its line—costs which the railroad in turn passed on to the United States government and the taxpayer. With the backing of Union Pacific board members, Crédit Mobilier decided to take the situation in hand by buying off a slate of key government officials, just to ensure no one looked too closely at all those receipts.[28]

The *Sun* revealed a handwritten list of thirteen congressmen who had been given Crédit Mobilier shares by one Oakes Ames, himself a Republican member of the House of Representatives from Massachusetts. The list was attached to a letter from Ames to another member of Congress, and included the names of James G. Blaine, the Republican Speaker of the House; Representative James Garfield, the future president; and Schuyler Colfax, then sitting vice president of the United States. It was the biggest bribery scandal in American history. Most historians have since concluded that Blaine was, in fact, not involved, and the House ultimately gave the others the barest slap on the wrist—Ames and one other member were censored, no one expelled—but the scandal sparked public fury and fear.[29] The railroad barons were trying to run the United States government. And who could stop them?

One House committee set up to investigate the scandal voiced the public's gathering discontent in a report issued a year later. "The country is fast becoming filled with gigantic corporations, wielding and controlling immense aggregations of money, and thereby commanding great influence and power," the report concluded. "It is notorious in many State legislatures that these influences are often controlling, so that in effect they become the ruling power of the State. Within a few years Congress has, to some extent, been brought within similar influences, and the knowledge of the public on that subject has brought great discredit upon the body."[30]

The railroad's influence in the federal government didn't stop with Congress. It extended all the way to the White House. Seventy-three men sat in the cabinet between 1868 and 1896, and of them, "forty-eight either served railroad clients, lobbied for railroads, sat on railroad boards, or had railroad-connected relatives."[31]

Suddenly the railroad barons were everywhere, extending their influence to every corner of the republic, to every jot of its business, buying legislatures, manipulating laws, installing themselves as the *aristoi*, the ruling elite, the de facto governors of the nation. And still they wanted more. In the closing decades of the century, the barons' determination to wring every last penny from their sprawling (and often outrageously mismanaged) empires ground their workers into poverty and led to a cascading series of labor strikes. Almost never willing to negotiate, the railroad magnates summoned state militias, hired and armed private soldiers, and on at least one occasion successfully demanded that the president of the United States deploy federal troops to put down the strikers. Hundreds died in bloody clashes.

The Great Strike of 1877 was illustrative. That year railway workers in Martinsburg, West Virginia, responded to the third wage cut in the space of a year by the Baltimore & Ohio Railroad by decoupling locomotives at the local station and leaving the trains to idle. Management refused to negotiate, and the strike spread from city to city over seventy days until it was forcibly ended by the National Guard at the direction of President Rutherford B. Hayes.

The very pattern was repeated year on year, across line after line, for two decades. Railroad ownership would slash wages and increase hours to boost profits, workers would then plead to be heard, and the barons would turn them away. In the company-owned town of Pullman, Chicago, the Pullman Palace Car Company had the audacity in 1894 to cut wages so brutally that its workers couldn't pay the rent on the company-owned lodging where robber baron George Pullman required them to live as a condition of advancement.[32] They launched a strike that temporarily halted railway traffic nationwide, before Attorney General

Richard Olney, who sat simultaneously on the boards of the Boston & Maine; the Eastern; the Chicago, Burlington, & Quincy; the Portland & Rochester; and the Philadelphia, Wilmington, & Burlington Railroads—all while serving in the cabinet—intervened.[33]

The public's sympathies were not always with the strikers, but they blamed the railroad barons above all. By the 1890s, the railroad magnates were, as historian Michael Hiltzik says, "anything but popular with their customers."[34] Disturbers of the peace, corrupters of government, agents of inequality; the barons had become symbols of all that troubled America. "Who own the United States?" one populist writer asked in the magazine *The Forum*. The answer: the capitalists and their families.[35]

Hated as they were, by the final decade of the nineteenth century the barons were struggling with massive problems of their own. Overbuilt and underfinanced, the railroads simply couldn't generate enough revenue to keep pace with costs. This quandary threatened to cripple the entire rail industry, and the American economy with it. This led the barons to their boldest gambit yet: an effort to reorganize the railroad business and the entire American economy around corporate monopolies.

■ ■ ■

What particularly incensed J. P. Morgan about Theodore Roosevelt's unexpected antitrust suit in the winter of 1902, laying aside the indignity and sheer disrespect of the thing, was Roosevelt's willful failure to see just how reasonable, how eminently necessary, monopolies truly were. Couldn't Roosevelt understand that unregulated competition between great companies was ruinous? You couldn't make any profit off it, not in the long run. And profit, well, good heavens, profit was the engine of progress. That's what Morgan believed. Which is why Morgan had done as he did and stopped the ridiculous and wasteful competition between two railroad magnates by bringing warring railroads under one holding company, the Northern Securities Company—controlled, it just so happens, by J. P. Morgan.[36]

That was precisely the sort of forward thinking the entire industry, nay, the entire country, required, Morgan thought.[37] The progress of industrial capitalism demanded it. In 1893, yet another panic on Wall Street sent the nation spiraling into depression, the latest trough in the cycle of bust and boom that plagued the last quarter of the nineteenth century. But this depression would last years. And it caught the railroad industry utterly unprepared. In 1893 alone, more than 640 banks failed nationwide, 5 percent of all banks in the country. Fifteen thousand businesses went bankrupt, including scores of railroads. By the end of the year, one-fifth of the nation's railroad track was in receivership.[38]

The railroads were overbuilt, there was no way around it. Hungry for the profits a successful railway promised and lured by sometimes lavish government grants and subsidies, railroad magnates had constructed more lines than the country could use, and often constructed them poorly. Once built, the only way to pay the bills, to maintain the enormous overhead and capital costs of running a rail operation, was to haul more freight and transport more paying customers than one's rivals, and to squeeze out every last efficiency while doing so. This competition led to a series of rate wars in the 1870s and 1880s, which saw multiple railroads go broke by slashing rates to outbid rivals. Over the same time period, the barons pursued efficiency mainly by cutting workers' wages. But the escalating resistance in the form of strikes and walkouts that those wage cuts provoked proved ultimately unsustainable. Tellingly, the one course of action the railroad barons were almost never willing to pursue was cutting their own rate of return, or that of their shareholders.

And so the railroads turned to . . . monopoly. It started with efforts to organize informal rate "pools" or pricing agreements, whereby rail lines sharing a single region agreed not to compete against each other directly, or agreed to set a price floor on their rates. J. P. Morgan tried to organize pools of this sort on more than one occasion in the 1880s, only to watch the agreements collapse when one or more of the competing barons reneged.[39] Now facing a tidal surge of bankruptcies and busts across the industry—and not just the rail industry, but across the entire industrial economy—Morgan and like-minded financiers hit upon a new approach. They would *combine* competing rail companies into giant corporations.

It seemed to make terrific financial sense. Outright consolidation allowed a railroad, or any industrial concern for that matter, to bring down costs by pursuing both vertical and horizontal integration—merging with one's suppliers, absorbing one's competitors—and to do it under singular, centralized management. It solved the sort of collective action problem Morgan had repeatedly encountered in trying to construct rate pools. It helped attract and control capital. And it achieved economies of scale. As one historian of the period has observed, "Given the expanse of the domestic market, and the ready access to it made possible by railway and telecommunication, the feasible optimum scale of industrial enterprise in the United States . . . far exceeded that in Britain and continental Europe."[40]

Thus began the greatest merger movement in American history. In 1890 the railroad industry, though giant in scale, still boasted an appreciable number of moderately sized, independent systems, fiercely competing against each other. A decade later, the independent lines had been swallowed up and metabolized by six mega-corporations that bestrode the rail industry like a colossus. Each of those was in turn controlled by its own small cabal. And J. P. Morgan was a cabal of one, with holdings totaling almost fifty thousand miles, valued at some $2.3 billion.[41]

What began in the railroads quickly spread to other industries. By 1904, "1,800 companies had been compacted into 157 behemoths in the steel, oil, tobacco, and copper industries and in gas, traction, and electric utilities."[42] In a flash, or so it seemed, the United States had gone "from a nation of freely competing, individually owned enterprises" to a country of corporate monopolies.[43]

From the capitalists' point of view, it all worked swimmingly. Financiers like Morgan made a killing reorganizing decrepit companies into new mega-corporations; there was so much organizing to be done, in fact, and so much money to be had doing it, that some investment banks abandoned their usual lines of practice to devote themselves to corporate restructuring. Morgan's own fee was reportedly $1 million per deal.[44] The corporate barons, meanwhile, delighted in the death of competition, or the diminution of it. One industrial economist from the time summed up their view: The terrible "waste of competition" could be "saved by combination of many manufacturing establishments in *one* industry under *one* management."[45] The new monopolies brought bulging profits without all that desperate competitive struggle. The capitalists were certain they had unlocked the secret of the industrial age. This was what the new economy, the new *country*, required, they decided: enlightened management and control, by persons such as themselves. And the corporate monopoly was just the vehicle to deliver it. It would be the miracle of the industrial age, the means for delivering America into a new and glorious future.

But not all Americans wanted to live in that future. Many spied in this supposed corporate nirvana, ruled over benevolently by the corporate barons, a political nightmare, a dystopia—a loss of independence, of self-government, of the republic itself. For in trying to change the deep structure of the American economy, the robber barons were in fact bidding to alter something more: the character of American life, and the political economy that had, up to then, sustained it.

■ ■ ■

The corporate monopoly was not unknown to the founding generation, quite the contrary. The citizens of the early republic knew it in the form of the famous and detested British East India Company, among other similar corporate instruments of the Crown. They feared such corporations as a menace to self-government. Corporations were by their nature instruments of concentration, putting wealth and privilege in the hands of a few. Corporations bred inequality—and that was death to a republic.

The early Americans believed republican liberty required not just a particular sort of government—one with free institutions responsive to the people—but a particular kind of society and economy. And they saw all three, government, society, and economy, as interlinked. For them, free government, republican government, was an *economic* choice as well as a political one. It required an economy where citizens of all stations could sustain their personal independence and live free of the control of any superior. Benjamin Trumbull of Connecticut put it this way in 1773: "For this purpose, it will be highly politic, in every free state, to keep property as equally divided among the inhabitants as possible, and not to suffer a few persons to amass all the riches and wealth of a country."⁴⁶ The founders' political science told them that independence was the lifeblood of a republic. Only if a man could stand on his own feet, win his own living, make his own way, could he participate as an equal in his government. And only if he had a share in self-government was he truly free. This was a way of thinking that the Americans inherited from their English forebears, a rich and venerable tradition—sometimes called republicanism—that stretched back to the city-states of the ancient world.

This same political worldview told the early Americans that a society turned aristocratic when the ambitious and upwardly mobile, the elite, amassed power and used it to reduce the working man to dependency. That was how republics fell. Here again, economic arrangements had political consequences. And by the same token, the founding generation believed politics shaped economics. The elite gathered power using politics—by writing laws and policies to their advantage. The early Americans did not believe that oligarchy was a *natural* development; they believed it was a *political* choice. That's where corporations came in.⁴⁷

Every state in the union banned the corporate form for private business in the early republic. States allowed it for churches, educational institutions, and other civic purposes, and they permitted it for public works projects overseen by the state itself, but not for private enterprise.⁴⁸ And this choice was entirely deliberate. As Supreme Court Justice Louis

D. Brandeis observed from the bench in 1933, the founding generation limited corporations out of fear: "Fear of encroachment upon the liberties and opportunities of the individual. Fear of the subjection of labor to capital. Fear of monopoly. Fear that the absorption of capital by corporations, and their perpetual life," might engender aristocracy and subvert the republic.[49]

Most states relaxed their bans on business incorporation in the 1830s and 1840s, but not because they had grown comfortable with monopoly. Rather, the public had grown disgusted with the abuses of *state-granted* monopolies, like the Second Bank of the United States, which Jackson-era Democrats argued had become an agent of aristocracy. The Jacksonians pressed for general incorporation laws as a remedy, to eviscerate the power of these state-sponsored monopolies.[50]

But in an irony of history, it was these very general incorporation laws dating back to the Jacksonian era, the ones adopted to root out monopolistic abuse, that J. P. Morgan and his capitalist set plucked up sixty years later and wielded to fashion the largest private monopolies in American history. They realized that to do so was to challenge the political science that had repudiated monopolies in the first place; it was to challenge the founders' republicanism. Morgan and company knew exactly what they were doing, and they did it openly. The founders' era had ended, they said. Their ideas were antique. Their fear of aristocracy was overblown. What America needed now was progress, and progress required the foresighted leadership of great men directing great business corporations. It required *combination*, in business, society, and government. Combination would be the watchword of the age, the path to the future.

The barons' arguments swept elite opinion in the course of a decade, such that by the early 1900s whole cadres of economists, academics, and like purveyors of conventional wisdom had decided corporate monopoly was the order of the day. It was *inevitable*. But out on the farms of the South and West, and in the factories of the towns, other Americans were far from convinced. In fact, they were alarmed—and angry—as the corporate barons swelled in power and prepared to engorge on the republic itself. In 1902, the dissidents found a champion in the youngest president in American history, Theodore Roosevelt, who was determined to make a stand for the old republic and the liberty of the common man.

CHAPTER 3

THE LAST REPUBLICAN

Theodore Roosevelt, the one-time rancher, writer, and hero of San Juan Hill, loved publicity, craved it, thirsted after it, and lived for it—and he had been expecting Pierpont Morgan that Saturday morning in 1902. He had expected it all: the stock market swoon, the blaring newspaper headlines. That was *the point*. Take a stand. Make the monopolists writhe. When Morgan did turn up, the meeting was brief. Still incredulous at the whole affair, Morgan suggested they settle things promptly, there, as between gentlemen. "If we have done anything wrong," he said to Roosevelt, "send your man to my man and they can fix it up." "That," Roosevelt responded, as he later gleefully recalled, "can't be done."[1]

By the time of the Northern Securities suit, Roosevelt had been president for a bare five months—since September 14, 1901, when William McKinley was struck down at the hand of an assassin. Roosevelt directed the attorney general to begin exploring antitrust action against Morgan and Northern Securities a short time later. It may still technically have been McKinley's term, but Roosevelt had never been a placeholder for anyone. This was a man who could start a war in the space of an afternoon, and very nearly did as assistant secretary of the Navy when his boss stepped out of the building (at which point Roosevelt famously cabled Commander Dewey to prepare to attack the Spanish fleet).[2] Now Roosevelt wanted war of a different kind, against the capitalist chieftains. He was determined to challenge their bid to install themselves as America's ruling class.

He saw in their campaign for corporate monopoly an attempt to change the nation's form of government, to convert it from a republic of the common man and woman into an elite-governed aristocracy, or maybe *plutocracy* was more accurate. "And of all forms of tyranny," Roosevelt would later say, "the least attractive and the most vulgar is the tyranny of mere wealth, the tyranny of a plutocracy."[3]

At the moment when it was under heaviest fire from the corporatists, Roosevelt stood by the founders' republicanism. He fought to preserve it for a new era. His efforts to do so were various and would change over the years. He started, as president, with stepped-up enforcement of the Sherman antitrust law. He went on to propose new corporate disclosure requirements to promote public scrutiny. In time, he would endorse even bolder and perhaps more dubious measures—direct federal control of all interstate corporations, including the power to set prices and issue stock.[4] But his aim was constant: to preserve what he understood as the promise of the old republic.

For him, that promise could be summed up in a single precept: government based on the dignity of the ordinary person, and under the ordinary person's control. "Our purpose is to increase the power of the people themselves," he would say, "to make the people in reality the governing class."[5] He believed liberty depended on the independence of the common man and on his capacity to share in self-government. He believed concentrations of wealth and power threatened the people's control and thus their freedom.

This is a perspective that in our day has almost entirely faded from view, sent into eclipse in no small part by Roosevelt's defeat in 1912. Roosevelt was the nation's last great republican. But it is a perspective worth recovering—vital to recover, in fact, as the basis of the American tradition of antitrust. And vital to understand as an alternative to the dull corporate liberalism that prevails today, the ideology fashioned by the last century's monopolists and their intellectual fellow travelers, the bipartisan liberalism that has dominated politics for decades and enabled the rise of Big Tech. Roosevelt's war against monopoly is a reminder of something different, of a different kind of politics that we might call to our aid in the modern fight against monopoly. And the key to understanding it is to understand the republican tradition's distrust of concentration, of *bigness.*

■ ■ ■

Roosevelt shared the earlier Americans' certainty that big concentrations of wealth and power were poisonous to a republic, absolutely deadly—because they were frequently the tools of elites, which is to say, aristocracy. Roosevelt was rehearsing a republican line when he argued that the "essence of any struggle for healthy liberty . . . must always be, to take from some one man or class of men the right to enjoy power, or wealth, or position, or immunity, which has not been earned by service to his or their fellows."[6] Every society had its elites, of course: its wealthy, well-educated, upwardly mobile types. Machiavelli, a republican himself, called them the *grandi.*[7] The trick to preserving a republic was not to allow them to predominate as a class, to amass power at the expense of their fellows. Or more precisely: the key was not to allow them to amass power at the expense of the common man.

Here we come to the heart of Roosevelt's and the American republican tradition's objection to bigness: elite, aristocratic concentrations threatened the power of the common man and woman. And the American republic, uniquely in history, set the common person at the heart of self-government. "Here we are not ruled over by others, as is the case in Europe," Roosevelt told an audience of cowboys in the Dakota Territory in 1886, "we rule ourselves."[8]

This was American gospel, or had been before the advent of the monopolists.[9] Liberty depended on the common person's power to share in self-rule. It's why Roosevelt would say the struggle for liberty was "the struggle of freemen to gain and hold the right of self-government as against the special interests."[10] It's why he would say the success of the republic depended on "the average man and woman": "just in proportion as the average man and woman are honest, capable of sound judgment and high ideals, active in public affairs . . . just so far, and no farther, we may count our civilization a success."[11] It is why he was opposed to monopoly and to great concentrations of power.

The republican tradition that Roosevelt and the early Americans inherited linked liberty to participation in self-government. It said that to be free depended on being able to share in self-rule, to have a say in society and politics.[12] It was not, in this respect, libertarian. It held that liberty was something more than the right to be left alone. This piece of the American heritage ran all the way back across the centuries to ancient Rome, a fact of which Roosevelt was very much aware: the example of the Roman republic—and its demise—was one he mulled for years.[13]

The Romans were great enthusiasts for liberty and, at one time in their history, dedicated practitioners of it. Even after the rise of the Caesars, the republic lived on in popular imagination and in political propaganda as a symbol of what it meant to be Roman.[14] Which was, in a word, to be *free*. The Roman citizen's boast par excellence, the thing that made him—and it was always a "him"—Roman indeed was his status as a free man, his ability to govern himself.[15]

The Romans had a firm idea about what that freedom amounted to. To their minds, to be free meant to be able to direct one's own destiny, to be the master of one's own fate, at no other man's mercy or command. No kowtowing, no begging for permission. Independent. Able to look any other man in the eye as an equal in worth, if not in wealth. In short, to be free was to be the exact opposite of those wretched slaves the Romans were always making of other people as they raged about the Mediterranean in their endless wars of aggrandizement.[16]

And here was the nub of it, the lodestar of the republican view. No man could be certain of his independence unless he had a say in the government of his nation. If some aristocrat, on a whim, could clap you into irons, or commandeer your land or cattle, then you weren't independent. And the only sure way to stop that happening was for you, you personally, to have some measure of control over who ran things. Because maybe the *grandi* were friendly today, very accommodating and liberal, but tomorrow—who could say? No, a man was only free if he had a voice in common affairs, if he was part of a free *state*. The Romans insisted those things went together, and had to: individual freedom and the freedom of the state—meaning the nation, the community of which you were a part. That was the whole idea of a republic. It was a state run by citizens who looked after their own interests, not a state run by an elite looking only after theirs.[17]

But conveniently for them, the Romans thought the citizen class was a rather elite group itself. Yes, citizens were in charge, but only the barest few persons qualified as citizens. The Romans, like most in antiquity, believed every person, every being, had its place—and those places did not change or move. They were what they were *by nature*. The slave was born to be a slave, the free man was born to rule. The cosmos was as a hierarchy, a pyramid, a beautiful, immovable ladder of status. And lest anyone be confused, the tippy-top rung was vanishingly small. The Romans may have waxed poetic about the liberty of a citizen, but they reserved citizenship for a tiny class of educated, freeholding males they believed were fitted *by nature* to be free, and thus to share in self-rule. Women, common laborers, slaves—none of these persons could possibly enjoy the status of citizen, because none were equipped by nature with the gifts and aptitudes self-rule required. The lesser was to serve the greater and be subordinate. That was the way of the world, the great order of being inscribed on the fabric of the universe itself.[18] Roman liberty, in short, remained an elite-driven affair.

While Theodore Roosevelt and the early Americans admired Roman republicanism, it was not their sole model of republican government.

They inherited a Christian strand of republicanism, too, one that came to them by way of James Harrington and the seventeenth-century English revolutionaries (Roosevelt would write an entire biography on one of these, Oliver Cromwell), but whose origins stretched back to the New Testament writings of Paul the Apostle, the man who was, in the words of historian Larry Siedentop, perhaps "the greatest revolutionary in human history."[19] What was revolutionary about Paul in a political sense was his insistence on the dignity of ordinary people and ordinary life.

Paul's writing announced an audacious new claim, very nearly unfathomable in antiquity. He said that the one almighty and sovereign God of the universe had intervened in world affairs for the purpose of saving, delivering, rescuing *every* man and woman. No matter their station, no matter their class. *Every* individual. Now, "save" meant many things, but not least of all it meant *claimed* by God and *energized* to become an agent of his divine purposes.[20] "Do you not know that your bodies are temples of the Holy Spirit, who is in you, whom you have received from God?" Paul asked one of his audiences.[21] The Holy Spirit was received by women as well as men, slaves as well as free persons, poor as well as rich, high-status Roman citizens and low-class social nonentities alike. This God was no respecter of persons. "Not many of you were wise by human standards," Paul emphasized in the same letter, "not many were influential; not many were of noble birth"—but all had received the power of God.[22]

In fact, Paul seemed to go out of his way to thumb his nose at the socially pretentious ruling elite of the Roman milieu. "God chose things the world considers foolish in order to shame those who think they are wise," he preached. "And he chose things that are powerless to shame those who are powerful."[23]

Choosing the weak, shaming the strong—Paul's gospel shattered the ancient world's studied and elaborate social superstructure. "There is neither Jew nor Gentile, neither slave nor free, there is no male and female, for you are all one in Christ Jesus," he claimed.[24] This was not to say those previous categories ceased to exist. It was to say they ceased to *matter* for one's worth, one's dignity.[25] And the political implications were massive.

Paul's teaching suggested that all those hopelessly *common* people the Roman patricians despised could be citizens too—that they were elected by God himself, instruments of the divine. And under pressure of this radical claim, this whole new point of view, the Roman notion of liberty began to shift. If the ordinary laborer could claim a stake in the republic; if his life, or hers, the life of sweat and soil and child-rearing, had significance, well—that would yield a republic of an altogether different kind. That would give you a commonwealth organized around the common person. That would mean the common life, ordinary life, would become the republic's chief end and goal, not glory or conquest or war. That would be a place where laborers were recognized as fit to govern, where labor itself was honored and the homely virtues of working life enshrined as the civic virtues of the nation.[26]

And that is largely what a group of English revolutionaries claimed in the seventeenth century, more than a thousand years after the fall of what remained of Rome, when they dusted off the old Roman theories of liberty to explain why a republic was the only government fit for free persons, a republic now redefined as the preserve of the common man. James Harrington, John Milton, Algernon Sydney—not household names in today's America, but significant nonetheless, because it was through their writing and practice that this reformed republicanism entered the American bloodstream.[27]

Indeed, this style of republicanism lived in the American mind from the republic's beginning, and shaped the American experience. You could hear it in the cadences of the American founders. There was Thomas Jefferson praising the working farmer, out in the field with his oxen and plow, the sort of man the Roman aristocrat wouldn't have given the time of day. "Cultivators of the earth are the most valuable citizens," Jefferson said. "They are the most vigorous, the most independant [sic], the most virtuous, and they are tied to their country and wedded to it's [sic] liberty and interests by the most lasting bonds."[28] At Jefferson's hand, the ordinary laborer had become the model citizen.

Then there is James Madison and his famous constitutional design, drawn up after an extended survey of ancient Roman republicanism and a thorough rereading of its English reformers.[29] The key to Madison's grand new system was the division of governmental powers into different "departments": legislative, executive, and judicial. And why? So that *the people* might exert control of government *for themselves,* and not be ruled over by any one elite or class, now rendered as "factions."

And thus did the republican suspicion of bigness, of monopoly, of concentrated power, and of elitism become part of American constitutional law—and American culture. This was the republicanism Theodore Roosevelt inherited, the tradition that told him monopoly was a thing to be feared and strictly controlled. This was the tradition that enshrined the inviolable liberty of the common man.

■ ■ ■

The question for Roosevelt was how to preserve this tradition against the revisionist campaign of the corporatists. The corporate barons argued concentration was natural and inevitable—more than that, it was salubrious, it was progress, it was the future. The economy could be organized by a well-informed few; there was no danger in economic aristocracy.

At first Roosevelt refused to yield an inch to bigness. Between 1902 and 1906, Roosevelt as president filed a bevy of antitrust suits against high-profile targets, beginning with J. P. Morgan's Northern Securities. Even as those suits progressed, however, he harbored grave doubts that antitrust prosecutions alone would suffice to rein in the monopolists. Antitrust prosecutions took time, often years, and were always backwards-looking—they focused on what offending corporations had done in the past, not how they might be regulated to address the menace they posed to free government going forward. In 1903, Roosevelt tested a somewhat different approach. He convinced Congress that year to adopt new transparency measures, including creating a Bureau of Corporations within the Commerce Department invested with authority to investigate potential monopolies (and other corporate misfeasance) and issue reports to the president.[30]

As his presidency progressed, Roosevelt came to believe the barons were half right. Corporate consolidation was perhaps inevitable, however unfortunate. But he resisted the notion that corporate monopolies should be allowed to manage the economy, or the new corporate class left free to pile up wealth and influence unchecked. He proposed an alternative path, one he believed to be in keeping with the republican tradition. The giant corporations should be subordinated to the power of the people through the regulation of the federal government. The American people "must effectively control the mighty commercial forces which they have themselves called into being," he declared, and he proposed to do it with federal power.[31]

As his presidency came to a close in early 1909, Roosevelt settled on an ambitious program of executive regulation. He proposed to require all corporations doing business in interstate commerce, which was all the biggest ones, to be licensed by the federal government and directly subject to federal oversight. On this scheme, no corporation could issue stock without federal approval, and the secretary of commerce would have authority to call in existing stock and issue new shares.[32] After he left office, Roosevelt added several more features to this program. He proposed to give the Commerce Department, or a new trade commission, the authority to unilaterally designate any corporation a monopoly, without first undertaking antitrust prosecution. The corporation could appeal the government's designation to a court, but the usual process would be reversed: the government could declare a monopoly *first*, and judicial process to review that decision would follow after. And on Roosevelt's plan, once the government had named a corporation a monopoly, it could invoke a range of new powers to regulate the corporation's business practices, methods of competition, and internal workings—including the setting of prices.[33]

This was Roosevelt's mature solution to the problem of corporate monopolies. It amounted to an effort to convert the major corporations into public utilities. One historian has called it "public-service capitalism."[34] Roosevelt had come to regard corporate concentrations as unavoidable, but he had not come to accept them. He wanted to curb their power by subjecting them to federal control, and in so doing head off a corporate aristocracy. In this manner, he hoped to secure to the common person, "the majority" of the nation, to "the farmers, and especially to the workers as the new rising class . . . the wealth commensurate with their weight in the body politic. . . ."[35] Roosevelt would advocate this program in his attempt to regain the White House as a Progressive in 1912.

He failed. As president, he could not persuade his own party to join his defense of the old republicanism. The Republican-controlled Congress never fully supported his antitrust suits, and it rejected his new regulatory program just as he left the White House. Out of office, he fared little better. Party brokers blocked his bid to win back the Republican nomination for president from William Howard Taft in 1912. So he ran as a third-party candidate on his plan of corporate regulation, but lost to Woodrow Wilson in a three-way race. And in truth, Roosevelt had by then probably conceded too much. His regulatory program tacitly accepted corporate bigness and attempted to neutralize its threat with bigger government, a path that posed dangers of its own. Roosevelt, however, never abandoned the germ of the founders' republicanism, the right of the common man to rule. And he never gave up trying to break the power of the corporate class.

His defeat in 1912 marked a watershed. Though far from politically conclusive—Roosevelt and Taft together outpolled Wilson, who in two presidential elections could never muster a popular majority—it was nevertheless seminal. For Wilson was not only uninterested in the founders' republicanism, he was hostile to it. He accepted the heart of the corporate barons' economic arguments, that monopoly was inevitable, normal, even *necessary*, and he went a step further: he articulated a new ideology of freedom to justify a corporatized society and the rule of the elite. Wilson was the nation's first prominent corporate liberal. And his victory in 1912 set the stage for all that was to follow, right up to the emergence of the globalizing, monopolizing Big Tech.

CHAPTER 4

THE TRIUMPH OF CORPORATE LIBERALISM

The robber barons' bid to remake the American economy around monopoly wasn't merely about economics, of course; it was about the whole of American life. The corporatists were proposing a wholesale replacement for the republican style of society that had characterized America from its founding, with its celebration of the common man. That was out, yesterday, passé. The barons advocated instead a new ideology that approved of bigness and concentrations of power in society and government. In place of the common man, it extolled the modern ideals of scientific expertise. It celebrated a social hierarchy based on education and wealth. It elevated a new professional class over labor. And it made the management of the American economy, no less than American government, the province of elites. This was corporate liberalism, and Woodrow Wilson arrived just in time to help bring it to power.

He did it by supplying the corporatists with a new and serviceable theory of freedom. The old republican ideal linked liberty with self-government by the common man, which is why the republican tradition insisted that bigness, concentrations of wealth and power, was a threat to freedom. The corporatists said all that was obsolete. Wilson explained why this was no problem: you could have corporate hierarchy *and* personal liberty. That was because, according to Wilson, liberty had no necessary connection to self-rule. Liberty was about making personal choices, about realizing one's own "individuality," as he would put it; it was a kind of self-expression.[1] The common man didn't require control over government or economic independence for that. On the contrary, this was a kind of freedom that government and the corporations working together could guarantee individuals. And that was precisely what Wilson proposed they do.

Wilson put his theories into practice. As president, he secured legislation to end the federal anti-monopoly efforts of Presidents Roosevelt and Taft and replaced them with a new trade commission that would promote a more cooperative approach, blessing the corporate order in exchange for regulation by new bodies of experts within the federal government. Indeed, Wilson worked to corporatize the government itself, to remodel its operations along the lines of the "modern" and "progressive" corporation. This newly active, newly expert government would secure the people's liberties—not by breaking up the monopolies or subjecting them to state control, but by guaranteeing the populace material prosperity and the right to pursue their life choices. This was the Wilsonian settlement, the triumph of corporate liberalism that would dominate America's politics and political economy for a century and reach its apotheosis with Big Tech.

■ ■ ■

Wilson entered politics comparatively late in life, after a full career in academia. He was never a particularly original scholar, but he spent enough time in the academy to absorb the prevailing ideas of the day, including a rock-solid belief in evolution, both biological and *social*. Wilson elevated Darwinism into something of a political creed, and that creed told him the founders' republican vision of liberty and economy was utterly outmoded. Wilson pronounced the republican ideal of independent producers—remember Thomas Jefferson's praise for the independent farmer, the most virtuous of citizens—as unrealistic, if not downright foolish. He dismissed the notion that it had any relevance for the modern era. "We live in a new and strange age and reckon with new affairs alike in economics and politics of which Jefferson knew nothing," Wilson said.[2]

He was similarly critical of James Madison. Wilson found Madison's republican-influenced constitutional design, the one that was supposed to check concentrated power and ensure the people's control, to be unwieldy, too rigid and difficult to use. It didn't promote positive government, he complained. That is, it didn't change with the times; it didn't evolve. The problem with Jefferson and Madison and the founders' political science generally was that it was "Newtonian" and mechanistic, Wilson said, rather than organic and evolutionary. It was forever trapped in the past.[3]

Wilson saw himself, by contrast, as a man of the future, a champion of progress. And he believed the new corporate order represented the progress the nation needed. "The life of America," he said in 1911, "is not the life it was twenty years ago. It is not the life it was ten years ago. We have changed our economic conditions from top to bottom, and with our economic conditions has changed also the organization of our life."[4] There was a time in American history when "corporations played a very minor part in our business affairs," but that day was past. "[N]ow they play the chief part, and most men are the servants of corporations."[5] The great corporations were the future, "the combinations *necessarily* effected for the transaction of modern business."[6]

Note the word "necessarily." Wilson regarded this new corporate dispensation as perfectly natural, more than natural, as *necessary,* because it was the outcome (he held) of historical evolution. Society was growing ever more complex and cooperative; it was progressing. The corporations were the economic manifestation of that progress. "We will do business henceforth when we do it on a great and successful scale, by means of corporations," he said.[7] The great business combinations represented a higher plane of evolution. "Society, in short, has discovered a new way of massing its resources and its power of enterprise": the giant corporation.[8]

Wilson's rhetoric in the final months of the 1912 presidential campaign has led some scholars to believe that he opposed the corporate reorganization of the economy, that he was a champion of "competition" and believed big business was a temporary phenomenon, perhaps reversible.[9] And indeed Wilson did sharpen his tone on monopolies after meeting in August 1912 with Louis Brandeis, an attorney, antitrust advocate, and later Supreme Court justice. But as Brandeis later supposedly remarked, Wilson never really understood bigness. Wilson's anti-monopoly rhetoric was mostly strategic, an effort to forge contrast between his ideas and Roosevelt's program of federal regulation. Wilson spoke of "regulated competition," a slogan he never fully elaborated but that implied a more laissez-faire approach, and he suggested that Roosevelt's federal regulation of monopolies would actually entrench them for good.[10] But it was Wilson who in fact accepted corporate bigness as not merely inevitable, but progressive—as an evolutionary fact of life to be embraced. And he accepted the corporate aristocracy that came with it.

"I am not afraid of anything that is normal," Wilson declared. "[T]he organization of business upon a great scale of co-operation is, up to a certain point, itself normal and inevitable."[11] And again: "Big business is no doubt to a large extent necessary and natural"; its development "is inevitable."[12]

The acid test was Wilson's response to the founders' republicanism, to their vision of the independent common man. And here Wilson left no doubt. He dismissed as hopelessly mired in the past those who, like the Populists and William Jennings Bryan within his own party, defended the republican vision. They wanted to reverse the course of social evolution, he said, which meant they wanted to turn back progress. "Most of our reformers are retro-reformers," Wilson said of this group. "They want to hale us back to an old chrysalis which we have broken; they want us to resume a shape which we have outgrown."[13] Wilson emphatically included Theodore Roosevelt in the same category. He regarded Roosevelt's fulminations against the robber barons, the "great malefactors of wealth," in Roosevelt's phrase, as so much tilting at windmills. "[T]hings that have happened by operation of irresistible forces," he said in 1912, are not "immoral things."[14]

There could be no resuscitating the founders' republican vision. The task now was to accommodate the rise of the corporation and the new shape it was bringing to society. That meant changing the country's laws to normalize the nascent corporate order, to embed it in the American regime. Wilson may have invoked "competition" from time to time, but he was clear even in 1912 where his real objectives lay. "Our laws are still meant for business done by *individuals*; they have not been satisfactorily adjusted to business done by great *combinations*, and we have got to adjust them," he declared. "There is no choice."[15] As president, that is precisely what he would do.

Yet Wilson recognized that before the emergent corporate regime with all its social implications could be made permanent, someone would have to explain why this new order was compatible with that most cherished of American ideals, liberty. If the republican liberty of the common man were to be swept aside, discarded as a relic of the past, something would have to take its place. Wilson set out to explain what that something was, with arguments that continue to reverberate into the present day.

■ ■ ■

To Wilson's mind, the most powerful agent of social evolution was the enlightened individual. His theory of freedom focused on producing that kind of morally evolved person. Wilson had been raised a Presbyterian, the son of a minister in the rural South. But he was no Calvinist, at least not in any traditional sense.[16] His father had considered himself a theological "liberal," and all that left Wilson with this: a lifelong belief in the perfectibility of human nature, which was to say, the human capacity for moral evolution. As an adult, Wilson would speak frequently of the human creature as a "fallen" being, but for him this was a metaphor for humans' tendency toward selfishness and error. Those deficiencies could be overcome, he thought; the human person could evolve toward moral perfection with proper training, education, and refinement.[17] What the individual needed was to be developed. He needed the occasion and opportunity to realize his moral potentialities. Individual development of this kind was vitally essential, not just for the person himself but for society: society's progress depended on it. Put another way, individual development powered social evolution.

"The hope of society," Wilson concluded in his last major academic work in 1898, "lies in an infinite individual variety, in the freest possible play of individual forces."[18] Individual forces: Wilson did not think for a second that each individual was alike, not in the least. He believed in no fixed human nature and no one expression of individuality. Human "perfection" was not one thing. It took many forms. Wilson believed in "*an infinite* individual variety" of personalities, of moral possibilities, and each individual had to be free to discover his or her potential—and develop it.

And here we come to what was, for Wilson, the essence of what it meant to be free. It meant to be able to achieve one's own individual personality, to pursue one's own self-development. "The individual," he said, "must be assured the best means, the best and fullest opportunities, for complete self-development."[19] No one person could say for another what his or her life was or should be. No one person could determine another's expression of personality. Individuals had to make their own way, to realize for themselves what their life might be, to achieve it—and in this way, to evolve toward perfection. For this was the meaning of life: to progress, to strive, to become oneself according to one's own lights. And all of this required *choice*. There must be "freedom of individual choice" in order for true freedom to exist, Wilson said. Only through exercising this power of moral choice, of moral self-discovery, of self-expression, could individuals be either "moral" or "free."[20]

And government had a role to play. Yes, this was in fact government's highest calling, the end and purpose of the state, "to aid the individual to the fullest and best possible realization of his individuality."[21] If there was a danger in the age of combination that Wilson otherwise celebrated, it was located just here, in the possibility that individuals would lose their power of self-realization, that it would be crowded out by the growing complexity of society. Organisms evolved toward complexity, of course—Wilson knew that from Darwin—so complexity was right, complexity was good. But the individual's power of self-development and choice had to be preserved amid all this complexifying. Wilson saw that as the central problem of liberty in the industrial age. "[W]e now realize that Americans are not free to release themselves," he told an audience in February of 1912. Too many Americans felt overwhelmed, their creative powers stultified. He promised a "release" of individual energies![22] Liberty was found in that release, in the power to shape one's own life and create one's own personality.

Here was a conception of liberty premised not on the control of the common man over his government, nor on his economic independence, nor on his power in society. This was instead a privatized, inward-looking notion of liberty that located freedom in the ability to make important life choices (however defined) and left the business of self-government to . . . someone else. In fact, Wilson's notion of liberty separated personal freedom from self-government altogether. Democracy had nothing necessarily to do with liberty, defined as Wilson was defining it. If liberty meant individual self-development, self-realization, the ability to discover one's own way, why, the rule of the common man might interfere with that liberty as much as the rule of any tyrant. Wilson said so. "I believe that the principal menace of a democracy is that the disciplinary power of the common thought should overwhelm the individual instinct of man's originative power," he wrote.[23] The rule of "common thought," of the common person, the common majority, must not be permitted to stifle the creative powers of the individual.

The idea that there was some connection between democratic participation and freedom was something the old republicans got wrong, Wilson thought. They confused the liberty of the individual with the form of the state. Liberty as the ability to pursue one's own ends, to craft one's own identity and pursue one's own life goals, made democratic participation seem rather beside the point. It might be a nice hobby, a pleasant pastime, perhaps educational in its own way, but it was hardly *essential* to liberty. Self-government and liberty were separate things.

All this explained why the emergence of the corporate economy, indeed of a corporatized society, was not to be feared after all. One didn't need to possess property of one's own, one didn't need to be financially independent from the capitalists, one didn't need to participate in self-government—as the old republicans had said—in order to be free. Freedom wasn't about property or political participation; it was about making personal life choices, such as defining one's moral code and pursuing personal happiness. Let the corporatists run the economy, let "most men" be the "servants of corporations," in Wilson's words.[24] None of that mattered—just so long as individuals enjoyed a sufficient modicum of prosperity to pursue their life goals.

Now Wilson certainly recognized that his idea of liberty as self-development couldn't be entirely divorced from economics: it would require some level of shared prosperity, lest all the grand talk of life choices turn out to be entirely hollow. If a citizen couldn't meet his basic needs for shelter and health, how was he to make anything of his life? And that's what government was for, in Wilson's view, to make sure the prosperity of the new corporate economy was broadly distributed. Government must see to "social convenience and advancement" in a new way, by spreading corporatism's benefits.[25] All that to say, individuals needed a decent living, yes; what they didn't need was *independence*. In Wilson's conception, it didn't matter how the bounty of the corporate economy came to individuals, whether from small, independent businesses (like family farms) or from the beneficence of the corporatists or from government, as long as it came.

Economic independence, so critical to the republican ideal, was written out of Wilson's theory.

By the same token, individual liberty did not depend on one's political participation in self-government. This too was a job that could be left to the corporatists or to their political equivalents, the expert class. Wilson, like the corporate barons, was a great believer in expertise and scientific management, and he wanted those qualities to rule the day in government. To address the monopoly question, for instance, which Wilson considered largely a matter of curbing the most outlandish corporate abuses and soothing public fears, he favored the creation of an expert commission, to be staffed by economists and other men of "science." That is, men who understood that "[w]ide organization and cooperation have made the modern world possible and must maintain it."[26] These were the people to take the trust question in hand. And he wanted to see this model, management by independent experts, replicated across the government. There was an implicit contrast here: the main point of having experts run the government was so that vulgar popular majorities would not. Wilson's approach reflected the corporatist faith in the rising professional class as opposed to the people of "common thought."[27]

The journalist Walter Lippmann, who supported Wilson over Roosevelt in 1912 and went on to serve for a time in the Wilson White House, drew out the implications of Wilson's teaching. "The public is interested in law, not in the laws; in the method of law, not in the substance," he said.[28] The republican idea that everyday citizens could ever know enough to run a complex and modern government in competent fashion was purest myth. It belonged to the legendary past, to the lost world of the "simple, self-contained community."[29] The *people* didn't need to run anything in order to enjoy liberty. They just needed to be properly provided for, to enjoy a basic standard of material comfort. That would be government's job. The rest could be left to the experts.

Wilson's privatized, choice-focused theory of liberty proved compatible with all this—and with the corporatization of *society* as well. The sharp corporate distinction between management and labor carried its own distinct social implications. On the corporate model, labor was no longer honored as independent, self-directing, and self-reliant. The republican ideal of the "sturdy yeoman" was dead. Labor was brawn, muscle work rather than brain work, little more than a dumb force of nature that become valuable only when expertly deployed by the management class. Earlier Americans had considered labor the source of all economic value; the independent laborer was the basis of the traditional republican political economy.[30] No longer. The corporate model said value came from management. It was the professionals, not the laborers, who were to be celebrated as the leaders of society (just one rung beneath the capitalists, naturally). Wilson had long believed that history was made by great men, those who rose above the rest, those with truly original minds.[31] The corporatist elevation of the professional and manager class was of a piece with this.

This social restructuring was the heart of the corporatist campaign as a *social movement.*[32] The corporate apologists offered a new vision for society in which the dignified, independent, self-sustaining laboring class, which the early Americans had believed to encompass most of the population, would be replaced by a new hierarchy: capitalists, educated professionals, and workers—now usually accompanied by the label "untrained"—in that order.[33] Labor was no longer to be the common lot of mankind; it was no longer to be regarded as essentially noble and ennobling. It was something to be escaped. And in place of the republican ideal of self-government by the laboring man, the corporatists offered a new ideal called social mobility—the chance to leave the (degraded) laboring class and become a professional. Or even, with some luck, a capitalist.

Harvard University president James Bryant Conant would sum up this new promise of the corporate society in a speech given several decades after Wilson won the White House.[34] Social mobility meant "careers freely opened to all the talented," he explained. That is, it meant a chance to rise out of labor and the lower social orders through the mechanism of "higher education." In other words, the professional class was open to those from any stratum of society, and higher education would recruit professionals from far and wide. This was "the essence of the American ideal of a classless" nation.[35] The professionals would still get top billing, mind you. The very terms of Conant's argument recognized the social hierarchy: social mobility meant the opportunity to rise *from* the working class *to* the professional, managerial one. "Mobility" was about the recruitment of elites.[36] In later years, it would go by the name "meritocracy," but amount to the same thing. The corporate reconstruction of American society had carried the day.

Corporatism as a social movement was, not surprisingly, a movement composed of elites, those with social standing—academics, professionals, and, of course, the capitalists themselves—people like Woodrow Wilson. And Wilson's privatized, choice-based theory of freedom helped the movement take hold. He said freedom could be found no matter who precisely governed the nation or who ran the economy; it was available to persons of all social strata. Freedom depended not on the right to participate in self-government or exercise social power, but on the ability to develop one's personal talents and make personal life choices. Indeed, the corporate reconstruction of America might actually aid freedom understood in this way. It would, Wilson hoped, provide greater prosperity that might be distributed more evenly by government. And that prosperity would underwrite Wilson's theory of liberty as private choice.

Wilson's theory sanctioned the reforming ambitions of the corporate party and linked them to the broad and deep American tradition of individual liberty. He would use this connection, and the rhetoric of liberty it afforded him, to great effect against Theodore Roosevelt on the campaign trail in 1912. "Theirs is a program of regulation," he said of Roosevelt's public-service capitalism, "ours is a program of liberty."[37] It was Roosevelt who was the innovator, Wilson charged, Roosevelt who wanted to alter fundamentally the shape of American life. Wilson was merely protecting individual liberty. This was individual liberty reconceived, of course, maneuvered away from the notions of independence and self-government toward private choice; it was individual liberty for the corporate age. But it served, in Wilson's hands, to explain why the corporate reconstruction of American life was not to be resisted, why it was not such a radical departure after all.

And in this way, and with his victory in the presidential campaign, Wilson helped deliver corporate liberalism to America. It was a new ideology for a new age. It approved of bigness, of concentrations of power in business and government, as essential to an evolving society. It idealized scientific management and expertise. It deprecated labor and installed a new social hierarchy that honored education, professional training, and access to capital. And it regarded liberty as connected not to self-government, but to private choice and self-development. Corporate liberalism was an ideology of the private market, not socialized government control, but it embraced a larger role for government in market regulation and in the distribution of wealth. And all of this was to be in service to the corporatized hierarchy of economy and society, to the rule of the elites.

■ ■ ■

Wilson's policies in office followed his ideas and cemented the arrival of corporate liberalism. Between 1913 and 1916, Wilson achieved a remarkable spate of legislative victories that, taken together, entrenched the new corporate order and removed the monopoly question from the foreground of American politics. His new antitrust legislation set up that regulatory body of economic experts that Wilson had advocated on the campaign trail, the Federal Trade Commission (FTC). It was charged with policing the market against unfair business methods and invested with power to subpoena records and persons, bring antitrust suits, and issue cease-and-desist orders. What it conspicuously did not do was what Theodore Roosevelt wanted: require corporations to be licensed by the federal government.[38]

The commission's powers were subject to judicial review, and the commission's mandate took its meaning from the Supreme Court's major antitrust about-face in 1911. That year, the court reversed course and declared that federal law barred not *all* restraints of trade—trusts, monopolies—but only "unreasonable" ones, in effect legalizing the great corporate mergers and returning the law to the status quo that had prevailed before Congress enacted the nation's first antitrust statute, the Sherman Act of 1890.[39] Wilson's legislation did not change this outcome, but merely gave the FTC enforcement authority within the court's parameters. The new FTC, then, emerged as a project to regulate and normalize the corporate behemoths rather than dissolve them. Its enforcement of the law was carried out "in a spirit of consultation with corporate officers . . . that might as often as not result in their entering consent decrees."[40]

In 1913, Wilson prevailed upon Congress to enact two other pieces of legislation long sought by the corporatists. His tariff reform bill sharply limited the protective tariff, the cornerstone of the national manufacturing policy for five decades. The corporations increasingly looked to markets abroad to expand, and their push for tariff revision demonstrated the new "international orientation of large corporate industry."[41] The corporate thirst for overseas markets and capital investment would henceforth play a major factor in American economic policy—by the Age of Tech, the dominant factor. That same year Wilson secured the Federal Reserve Act, creating a new national bank largely free of political control that would help stabilize capital markets and regulate the money supply in a manner to facilitate the corporate reorganization of the economy.[42] These changes were followed by enactment of the income tax to replace lost tariff revenue and to provide a dependable source of funding for government's expanding size and regulatory role. With the advent of the income tax came the start of a long-term shift from the taxation of capital to the taxation of labor.

The corporate order had fully arrived. Wilson's legislation had the effect of normalizing it and removing corporate questions, for a time, from political contention. He gave the nation a corporatized, increasingly globally oriented economy and a government to match. His new regulatory commission allowed him to talk tough about the trusts and punish select corporate misbehavior, but in a way that permitted corporate consolidation to go forward. The Supreme Court made this easier by dramatically limiting the reach of the Sherman Act in 1911. Wilson could claim, rightly, that he was enforcing the antitrust laws, without having fundamentally to upset the corporate regime. His other legislation made the corporate order stronger and more permanent.

With Wilson, the antitrust project's taproot in republican political economy had been cut. Presidents after him would take up the antitrust banner from time to time; Franklin Roosevelt did so notably in his so-called Second New Deal.[43] But these later antitrust efforts would not be linked to republican ideals and were rarely sustained for any length of time, and no wonder. Corporate liberalism offered no principled objection to bigness. Concentrations of power and wealth were inevitable, natural, even necessary for economic growth and prosperity. This was the new conventional wisdom. And from Wilson forward, this corporate liberalism was the order of the day.

Both Left and Right embraced it. Both camps would accept the corporate, global economy, though they proposed to manage it in different ways at different times. Both would accept the corporate liberal notion of freedom, of liberty as private choice to be guaranteed over and against the intrusions of the community and majoritarian democracy. And both Left and Right agreed on the basic political economy this idea of freedom generated. They agreed that liberty necessarily encompassed the right to enjoy material prosperity. The Right, to this end, emphasized the power of the private market. At their hands, the corporate liberal idea of a right to private choice became increasingly the right to market choice, and right-wing politicians celebrated the private market no matter how corporatized or consolidated it became. The Left, meanwhile, pressed the need for social welfare and redistribution of wealth, and over the decades steadily expanded the size and scope of the federal government for those purposes. Both political camps would accept the social order that corporate liberalism imposed, the ascent of the professional class and the "meritocracy," and the social devaluation of labor. These became the social landmarks of twentieth-century America that defined American politics.

Far from weakening over time, this corporate liberalism seemed only to gain strength as the years went by. The multinational corporation became more powerful, the economy more globalized, the divisions between the working and professional classes more profound and permanent. But then, from the electorate, came stirrings of discontent. For reasons the chattering class couldn't quite pinpoint, couldn't quite comprehend or even describe, the voting public became more and more out of sorts as the twenty-first century dawned, more resistant to the usual political platitudes and talking points. All the talk about market choice and lifestyle options began to sound somehow detached and unreal. Americans told pollsters that they felt they were losing control of their country, that their voices were unheard or disparaged, that they had no real power anymore over their lives. They felt at the mercy of government bureaucrats and global corporate managers.

And just then came the rise of Big Tech, the successors of the first robber barons, rehearsing corporate liberalism's rhetoric and redoubling its promises. But in a fitting dialectic, Big Tech's ascendance ended up forcing a more fundamental question to the fore: whether the corporate liberal order was worth preserving after all.

PART II

CHAPTER 5

ADDICTING AMERICA

When Facebook went public in May of 2012 in what was billed as the initial public offering of the decade—the century!—the company dutifully filed a dutifully boring piece of paperwork known as the Form S-1 registration statement, a compendium of facts and figures, summaries and disclosures, a "risk factors" analysis, "selected consolidated financial data," "description of capital stock," and so on and so forth.[1] Except this Form S-1 wasn't boring in the least. This Form S-1 was positively fascinating. This Form S-1 included a thesis statement direct from Big Tech on the new world the technologists hoped to create. It included a letter from Mark Zuckerberg.

Zuckerberg had put pen to paper (so to speak) and in the span of four brief pages attempted to explain to the vast public just what was before them in this dawning Age of Tech. For the world stood again on the precipice of transformation, Zuckerberg wrote, a transformation as profound as the one occasioned by the arrival of the printing press centuries before. That earlier technology "led to a complete transformation of many important parts of society," Zuckerberg said. And now "our society has reached another tipping point."[2] That's where Facebook came in. "Facebook was not originally created to be a company" at all. Rather: "It was built to accomplish a social mission. . . ."[3]

The ambition fairly leapt off the page. Like the corporate barons of the Gilded Age, Zuckerberg and his fellow technologists aimed at nothing less than the remodeling of American life. Past technologies and their inventors had "changed the way society was organized," Zuckerberg wrote. Now Facebook would do the same. And this renovation would be achieved by the advent of a new kind of economy, an information economy, built on (supposedly) the free flow of data. Tech would lead the way. It would make the country—indeed, the world—"more open and connected."[4] It would leverage the wide availability of the internet and mobile platforms to create an economy of "authentic businesses" built on "personalized" designs and products. It would deliver a "more open culture," "better understanding" between citizens, and "expos[ure] to a greater number of diverse perspectives." And all this would be done with data—massive amounts of data gathered from ordinary citizens and analyzed by the supercomputers at Facebook: data so prodigious one would need miles of computer servers to contain it, yielding analysis so precise that it could *predict* what consumers would want before even they knew it. This was the future, an economy and society based around data and those who controlled it, namely, Facebook and the other avatars of Big Tech.

Zuckerberg spoke of change, a fresh departure from the past, but in fact his pitch was the climax of the revolution his robber baron predecessors had initiated a century before. It was the climax of corporate liberalism. The grand future Zuckerberg envisaged was a future controlled by the few companies sufficiently large and powerful to collect massive amounts of information from consumers and put it to use. It was a future organized around the priorities of the cosmopolitan professional class: "openness" and "connection." In a later letter to Facebook users and employees, Zuckerberg spoke of building a "global community."[5] The twenty-first century corporate elite hail global integration—social, political, and economic—as the great engine of progress. They prize transnational ties over any distinctly American identity, and the new society they want to build reflects their globalist preferences.

Given the business scale required to succeed at the massive data extraction and control that the Big Tech agenda required, the companies that managed it would almost by definition become monopolies. In the words of technologist Jaron Lanier, "large, highly automated businesses" built around prodigious data collection "can't help but present some of the problems of monopolies."[6] The Age of Big Tech, like the age of the robber barons, would be the age of monopoly.

And it would be the age of addiction. Zuckerberg promised that Facebook would hasten the arrival of a better America by putting more information into the hands of more people than ever before. In fact, the truly transformative thing about Big Tech was its business model. Big Tech treated its users as sources of information to be mined and as objects to be manipulated. And the key to both was attention. Big Tech needed as many Americans online as possible for as long as possible, all in order to extract their personal data and manipulate them into buying the wares of Big Tech's advertisers. Far from empowering ordinary people, Big Tech assaulted their agency and undermined their independence. By design. This model doubled down on the legacy of last century's corporatists: elevating an ever-narrower group of professionals at the expense of ordinary citizens, consolidating power—and now information—in the hands of a few.

But there was no need to look too closely at what precisely Big Tech was about because, according to Zuckerberg, the reign of Big Tech would bring the people more of what every American wanted: liberty!—where liberty meant private, personal choice. This rhetoric, too, sounded in the cadences of corporate liberalism. "Think about what people are doing on Facebook today," Zuckerberg had enthused before the company went public. "They're keeping up with their friends and family, but they're also building an *image* and *identity* for themselves, which in a sense is their brand."[7] It was Woodrow Wilson's language of self-development transposed into a twenty-first-century key. Facebook would empower individuals to create—their own image, their own identity, their own personhood. More choice! More liberty! Yet in this version of corporate liberalism, as in the earlier one, the corporate elite and the professional class would be the ones with the power.

Big Tech was the robber barons' dreams realized; it was corporate liberalism's triumph. And while Zuckerberg was perhaps Big Tech's most avid evangelist, the other tech platforms shared Facebook's transformative aspirations and trafficked in the same soaring, Wilsonian rhetoric. Explaining why people used its famous search platform, Google opined that many searched "to fulfill the need for ongoing personal growth," still others to "develop and reinforce a sense of identity." This, Google attested solemnly, "is a powerful, emotional payoff of search."[8] Search queries on the internet could be a portal to self-fulfillment.

But if the key to the earlier corporatists' ambitions was their elevation of the giant, hierarchical monopoly, the key to Big Tech's plans was the business model of data extraction. In the words again of technologist Jaron Lanier, "The primary business of digital networking has come to be the creation of ultrasecret mega-dossiers about what others are doing, and using this information to concentrate money and power."[9] This was the new economy Big Tech would give America, and it depended centrally on capturing and controlling Americans' attention.

■ ■ ■

In 2011, 46 percent of Americans reported that they owned and used smartphones, those small, shiny portals to the internet.[10] By 2019, that number had rocketed to 81 percent, and the trend line was ever upward.[11] That same year, 81 percent of Americans said they spent time online "every day." And 28 percent said they were online "almost constantly." Break that last number down by age, and the results became even more vivid. Nearly *half* of eighteen-to-twenty-nine-year-olds said they spent the day "constantly" online.[12]

All of which spelled potential profit, if you knew where to look for it. Someone who did was Hal Varian, an otherwise obscure economist at the University of California, Berkeley, who had the enormous good fortune to end up as a senior economic advisor to a technology company called Google.[13] Or maybe it was Google that was fortunate, since Varian is the one who showed the company how to turn its users' attention into cash.

In a seemingly humdrum paper for the *American Economic Review* in 2010, Varian methodically laid out a series of observations that, taken together, formed the basis of the Big Tech business model, the *addiction* model.[14] Varian began with the central fact of modern technological life. Nearly every person spent copious amounts of time online every day. And as a consequence, between every individual's interactions with the world there now stood—a computer. Take commerce as just one example. "Nowadays," Varian pointed out, "most economic transactions involve a computer."[15]

Computers, of course, took many forms. "Sometimes," Varian said, "the computer takes the form of a smart cash register, sometimes it is part of a sophisticated point of sale system, and sometimes it is a Web site. In each of these cases, the computer creates a record of the transaction."[16] The record-keeping function was, in fact, the purpose of involving computers in the first place. But that was old news. Computer-mediated buying and selling opened a whole new realm of possibility for other things, like gathering information.

Varian explained: "[N]ow that these computers are in place," he wrote, "they can be used for many other purposes." Those purposes prominently included "facilitat[ing] personalization" and performing "data extraction and analysis."[17] What might that mean, in plain English? It meant that the online experience was now an opportunity for the owners of the computers—the big computers, the ones that ran the platforms—to gather information from unsuspecting private individuals. That is, their users.

"In the last 20 years or so, the field of machine learning has made tremendous strides in 'data mining,'" Varian observed.[18] Which meant that while the casual user was online, minding his or her own business, Google and Facebook could now follow her around to observe *everything* she did. Everything. And not just while she was visiting their platforms, but on other sites too. All day long.

It worked like this: An individual decided to sign up for a Google account, created an online profile, and Google surreptitiously slipped a "cookie"—essentially a miniature tracking device—onto her computer. After that, Google used this cookie to monitor its customer's movement online, including the names and URLs of websites she visited, the terms she searched, the videos she watched on YouTube. Everything. Internet browsing had become a rich opportunity for personal surveillance. Wherever Google or Facebook's users went, whatever they did, a computer was there, watching, recording, filing away information, listening in. (Today Google regards cookies as yesterday's tech—mostly because its rivals use them—but the strategy remains the same even as the technology continues to change.)

And the user meanwhile had—no idea. None at all. This was the beauty of "computer mediated transactions." No one noticed the mediator. The computers were so ubiquitous, so ever present, that no one even realized they were there. No one noticed that Google and Facebook and Twitter and Amazon were essentially giant computers, whose primary purpose was to monitor their customers' every move.

But didn't these companies have some obligation to alert their customers, to notify them, about this surveillance? In a word, no. Not in any meaningful way. While the platform giants *might* make passing mention of the *possible* monitoring that might *hypothetically* occur should customers use their platforms and services, these so-called disclosure notices were nearly impossible to understand and always underinclusive. They never told the user just what the surveillance truly amounted to or entailed.

A group of teachers from my home state of Missouri learned this firsthand. A few years ago, one of the larger public school districts in the southwest part of the state signed a contract with Google. By its terms, the company agreed to supply Google computers—called Chrome-books—as well as personal email accounts to students and their teachers. Teachers and students were also to get access to Google's web-based calendar, word processing, spreadsheet, and file storage applications. Google called this set of products the "education suite," and the company made the same offer to school districts around the country. Thousands of school districts said yes. By 2020, more than 80 million educators and students—more than half the students in the nation—used the education suite of products.[19]

But then teachers in Springfield, Missouri, discovered Google was doing something the general public knew nothing about, something no parent or teacher had expected. The teachers alleged Google was using its "education" products to spy—on the teachers, on the students, and on their families. And Google was doing it without the school district's knowledge and despite its best efforts, and without anyone's consent.[20]

According to a lawsuit in another state detailing Google's usual practices, Google would issue each teacher and student a username and password, and encourage users to sign into their new accounts both on their Chromebooks *and* on their personal, non-Google devices, like phones and home computers.[21] That was critical, because when they did, Google began monitoring users' every move and action.[22] Google appeared to track the websites they visited, their online searches, their personal contact lists, their physical locations, their voice commands. One Springfield teacher believed that Google had captured and stored each of her passwords to each of her online accounts, numbering 139 in all, from her personal bank account to her personal health portal.[23]

Worse, Google appeared to be using this highly personal and sensitive information to bombard students and teachers with advertisements, turning unwary users' most proprietary data into an opportunity for profit. Google's profit, naturally.[24] As for the advertisements, some students reported seeing, shall we say, indecent material in ads following school online research assignments for things like urinary tract infections.[25]

Google's algorithms made note of what the student searched and the sites she visited, made note of what material she clicked on or even lingered over, made note of her location and time of day, and then directed advertisements to her on the basis of all that information put together.[26]

In its contracts with schools, Google did disclose, in fine print, that with a password teachers or students could prevent Google from reading their sensitive data. But even this limited privacy option was turned off by default and concealed in settings that parents would likely never see.[27] All of which left users either in the dark or out of luck, and Google free to roam. And it is free. A federal judge recently accepted Google's claims that its cryptic, obscure privacy disclosure and opt-out were sufficient, arguing "there is no requirement that the notice be written in terms understandable by a child under the age of 13."[28] The opinion was a fitting summary of the state of children's online privacy in America.

The customers' loss of control meant more opportunity for Big Tech. The term data mining "was once pejorative," Hal Varian said in his paper, "but now enjoys a somewhat better reputation."[29] That was putting it mildly. Data mining, as in constant, ongoing, unseen surveillance, was to become the very lifeblood of the tech industry. And the reason was that this insistent surveillance permitted platforms to build vast new stores of information on their customers, and on potential customers, and on almost every person living, stores of information so vast the supercomputers behind the platforms could begin to *predict*, using millions of data points, what an individual customer would click on, watch, and buy. The supercomputers would know what a given individual with a given set of characteristics was virtually certain to do even *before* she visited Google or signed up for Facebook.

That was power. These platforms now had the ability, using data harvested from hundreds of millions of users and analyzed by proprietary algorithms, to predict accurately how individuals would behave, *before* they behaved at all. As one Google user exclaimed, "Google knows the REAL ME! . . . To tell you the truth, it probably knows me better than I know myself.[30] That was precisely the idea. Based on this vault of information and formulae, Google needed only to learn one or two things about you, the user, in order to forecast with astounding accuracy what you might do next. This was the power of "computer mediated transactions."

And that power, that capability, could be used for all sorts of commercial purposes, "an insurance company, a derivatives fund, a search engine, or an online store," for example.[31] But one of the most direct and profitable uses was the one Hal Varian helped Google pursue: online advertising.

Hard as it is to fathom now, when Google was founded in 1998 by two Silicon Valley Ph.D. students, it very nearly didn't survive. The world had search engines already. Yahoo!, for instance, had been founded four years earlier. Google's rhetoric was lofty—its founders, Larry Page and Sergey Brin, rehearsed all manner of high-minded verbiage about empowering the consumer, including a diatribe against too much advertising on search engines![32] But Silicon Valley was brimming with that kind of talk at the time. What Google conspicuously lacked was a way to make money. That is, until Hal Varian showed up, and Page and Brin discovered his "computer mediated transactions."

That changed everything. Armed with Varian's insights, the Google founders revisited their scruples. Ads were suddenly the future. Now when customers came to Google's search bar to type queries, Google didn't just answer their questions and let them go. No, it followed these customers around the internet (without their knowledge, of course). And using the information it found, Google developed a formula, a series of mathematical algorithms, for predicting which consumers would click on which ads, which customers would make purchases, and what they would buy.[33]

It was a remarkable breakthrough. For Google. With its massive and ever-growing store of user information, the company could direct tailored ads to individuals that its data machine suggested would have a high probability of leading to a purchase. Which in turn led to profit. Google had become the essential facilitator between advertisers and consumers. By tracking its users' every move, Google had accidentally invented advertising nirvana: a method for tailoring ads to push individual consumers toward buying.[34]

Having discovered this golden goose, Google set it to work. Google reoriented its entire product line for purposes of extracting maximum amounts of data from its users (still without telling them) and creating maximum opportunities for targeted, predictive, behavior-changing advertising. Across its vast array of products, the company painstakingly designed each new tool to gather every possible scrap of information from users and act as a conduit for these new data-driven ads. Soon enough, customers got so inured to the invasive tracking they started buying Google-branded listening devices and GPS trackers. You may know them as Android phones.

To keep the criticism at bay, Google made a big show every so often of revising these surveillance practices with one or two of its products, careful to leave itself enough wiggle room to keep snooping across its broader product line. In 2017, for example, Google announced to great fanfare that it would cease scanning users' emails for ads. After thirteen years of rifling through users' inboxes, it had the information it needed. And it had plenty of means to collect more. As one report noted, "The move to end targeted advertising in Gmail doesn't mean users won't still see ads. Google can still parse search histories, YouTube browsing, and other Chrome activity as long as you're signed into your Gmail account. But for those who might have been wary of Google's ad-targeting practices in the past, this may put those worries to rest. The company certainly hopes it will do so for potential corporate clients."[35] Surveillance had become Google's stock-in-trade.

■ ■ ■

But it was Facebook that took the possibilities of "computer mediated transactions" to an entirely different level. Before taking the company public, Mark Zuckerberg and fellow Facebook executive Sheryl

Sandberg, the latter formerly of Google, had a startling realization. Facebook possessed more data on more individuals than any company on planet earth. Those Facebook user profiles and friend lists were a data treasure trove. Whom did users know? Whom did they care about most? Whom did they trust, and whom could they be made to pay attention to? Layers and layers, veins and veins, of personal data. Each an opportunity to extract and to manipulate the substance of users' social interactions. Where Google could learn, and perhaps alter, what users thought, Facebook could see and shape what users *said*.

Zuckerberg's lieutenant, Sheryl Sandberg, understood that Facebook's opportunities were unique. "This isn't search and it's not monetization of search—that's direct response," she told industry watchers, referring to the then-conventional "pay for eyeballs" ad model. "We do see a huge opportunity in performance and brand marketing."[36] Thanks to its role as an intermediary between users' social interactions, Facebook marketers could, in the words of one industry observer, "insert themselves into that swap of information."[37] It could meme its advertisers' brands into users' heads, thanks to its unique trove of social data and power over the flow of social information. Who wouldn't pay for that kind of power?

Under the inspiration of Varian's data-mining, constant-surveillance model, Facebook leveraged its data on individual users to "personalize" their online experience, to make the platform interface feel unique, tailored, bespoke. Facebook set out to personalize everything it could. The users' "News Feeds" and "Timelines" of posts and comments were based on the personal data Facebook was constantly and secretly amassing—all for the purpose of claiming the users' attention.

Facebook realized the more personalized it made the digital experience, the more time users spent online. And the more time they spent online, the more information Facebook could quietly extract and the more advertisements it could sell. The point of Facebook's customization crusade was not to improve the user experience—the basic product Facebook has offered consumers has barely changed in a decade—but to keep users online and on Facebook *longer*.

Given the sums of money at stake, given the potential for profit, profit, and more profit, the tech companies could take nothing for granted when it came to keeping users' attention. It was an attention arms race. The platforms needed more attention, all the time. Tristan Harris, a former Google designer who was featured in the documentary *The Social Dilemma*, described Big Tech's aims this way: the goal was to make its products as addictive as a slot machine, and then to "put a slot machine in a billion pockets."[38]

Big Tech's engineers deliberately exploited users' conscious and unconscious "psychological vulnerabilities . . . in the race to grab [their] attention."[39] They deployed techniques like "intermittent variable rewards" to hook users' interest, little attention-grabbers that popped up when you checked your phone or signed into Google or Facebook, things like red badges and push notifications, combined with noise alerts and colors.[40] The object was to make users feel rewarded when they engaged with the platform so that they would do more of it.

As Harris explained, "When we pull our phone out of our pocket, we're playing a slot machine to see what notifications we got. When we pull to refresh our email, we're playing a slot machine to see what new email we got. When we swipe down our finger to scroll the Instagram feed, we're playing a slot machine to see what photo comes next."[41] All by design.

And just like the casinos—well-lit twenty-four hours a day to keep the players perked up, drinks flowing to loosen inhibitions—the social media architects were interested in controlling their users' moods. Deeply interested. In 2012, Facebook conducted a massive behavioral psychology experiment on 700,000 unwitting users—scientists would call them "test subjects"—to see if it could change how its users were feeling. They did it by tweaking the frequency with which subjects saw pleasant or unpleasant content in their feeds. It was billed as an academic contribution, very high-minded, to a field called "emotional contagion." And it worked. When Facebook showered users with negative content, the users' statuses reflected what they'd seen. They got bummed out. Or worse. One legal scholar summed up the experiment's goal well: "We wanted to see if we could make you feel bad without you noticing. We succeeded."[42] And it wasn't a one-off success.

The platforms quickly developed other techniques, more strategies to exploit the human species' need for social approval and our bent toward reciprocity. Facebook, for example, began encouraging users to name or "tag" other individuals they knew in group photographs. When you got tagged in someone else's photo, you got alerted: a little shot of social recognition. The bet being that with that little recognition, that little adrenaline shot of status, the recipient would be eager to log onto Facebook and do more posting of her own, to win more recognition.[43] "Imagine millions of people getting interrupted like this throughout their day," Harris reflected, "running around like chickens with their heads cut off, reciprocating each other—all designed by companies who profit from it."[44]

But it wasn't enough to give users more of the things they liked and wanted. As the attention arms race accelerated, platforms like Facebook needed to get users to read and watch things they didn't want, or didn't *know* they wanted before Big Tech helped them along. That's what features like "infinite scroll" were for, to keep users scrolling down—no end in sight. Always more to see, read, digest, react to. Google's YouTube pursued the same strategy, introducing its Autoplay feature for videos and media. Rather than waiting for users to make a conscious *choice* to consume more, these autofill features pressed additional content on the user, over and over again, no questions asked, no pause allowed, more attention required.

Users might have thought they were getting the latest information from their friends and their feeds when they signed into these services, but the platforms knew better. As they iterated their design, chronology—that simple, clean, impartial metric that might best serve users logging on to find out what's up—went out the window. Relevance was what would keep users hooked. Relevance is what would give the platforms control. The tech journalists went gaga for these innovations. "The big change Facebook announced today is that now, when you come back, Facebook's story scoring and ranking algorithm will look at all of the stories you have never seen, not just the stories created since you last visited," one professional stenographer announced. "In practice, that means if there was a story in your News Feed before, but you missed it because you didn't scroll down to see it, Facebook will put it up top the next time you visit the site if Facebook believes that story is more relevant to you than all the new ones created since you last checked the site." It was so lovely, so convenient, so . . . manipulative.[45]

Attention, attention, attention—with the help of Hal Varian, the platform giants had become attention-sucking, behavior-manipulating machines. And the results, that is to say the commercial rewards, were prodigious. Facebook and Google raked in billions, eventually tens of billions in profits, every single year.[46] That was something Wall Street could get behind. And it did, giving Facebook and Google some of the largest market capitalizations in the world.

All that attention and all that money gave those platforms something more. It gave them power. Power unheard of in American life, unseen in American history. No other corporations in the world had ever been able to take hold of their customers like these corporations did, to invade their very cerebrums, to watch them and track them and predict their behavior, to shape it. This was unprecedented power gained without consent or meaningful permission of any kind. And it was held in the hands of a precious few—the founders, foremost, the Zuckerbergs and Larry Pages and Sergey Brins of the world, and their entourage of executives. And then shared, derivatively, with the class of engineers and computer scientists and other professionals who had the good fortune to work with Big Tech or near it, or who worked in professions that benefited from the Big Data business model Big Tech pioneered.

This was the modern equivalent of the Gilded Age division between corporate management and labor. Those who worked with or near Big Data, or benefited from it, now stood at the apex of the socioeconomic scale. Those, meanwhile, who worked in old-fashioned industries that made actual things or in services not reliant on data found themselves increasingly shunted to the bottom of the hierarchy. In fact, the Big Tech economy depended on *taking* value from these people, ordinary people, to fuel the Big Tech data machine.

Like Wilson's corporate liberalism, which promised a "ladder" upward from mere worker to manager, Big Tech's deprecation of the real world and the real economy promised new forms of ascent—for the elect—from the rote work of the physical world to management of the digital systems that controlled it. "Today," blogger Venkatesh Rao observes, "you're either above the API [application programming interface] or below the API. You either tell robots what to do, or are told by robots what to do. To crash through the API, and into . . . the Jeffersonian middle class, is to go from being predator to prey in the locust economy."[47]

But how to crash through? The answer held out by Big Tech: become a content creator, a social influencer. YouTube didn't just give influencers a cut of ad revenue; it shipped them plaques. These promises have already transformed the aspirations of the next generation. According to a survey by Lego, 29 percent of American kids dream of becoming YouTubers, triple the number who want to become astronauts.[48] Meanwhile, digital marketing became a career path for go-getters, giving them a direct line to the new power elite, the decision-makers at the tech giants themselves, or at least their ad account managers. And maybe, just maybe, with a Google business card in the pile, a job interview at one of the big tech companies would come someday.

That fancy Big Tech job with that hefty Big Tech salary wasn't just a pipe dream, tech promised. Tech knew that those jobs were important to its sales pitch to the nation and its leaders. All the manipulation, the extraction, would be intolerable if there weren't some upside to American workers. When Mark Zuckerberg came to see me on Capitol Hill, he started our meeting by offering that Facebook intended to set up data centers in the Midwest, my home region. This point was in service to the Big Tech line that its industry can offer jobs to ordinary people, those without advanced engineering degrees or computer science training. But as Jaron

Lanier points out, "[T]he latest waves of high-tech innovation have not created jobs like the old ones did. Iconic new ventures like Facebook employ vastly fewer people than big older companies like, say, General Motors." Instead, Big Tech "channel[s] much of the productivity of ordinary people into an informal economy of barter and reputation, while concentrating the extracted old-fashioned wealth for themselves."[49]

This was the new-model economy Zuckerberg and Big Tech wanted to give the nation, not an economy of production and labor, but a digital "information economy" that rewarded those few who controlled the information and treated everyone else as objects to be manipulated.

This is not a world a free people would choose for themselves. Consider some of the modern horrors we are told we must accept: A private market of "data brokers" trafficking in personal data so sensitive that bounty hunters can purchase phone geolocation information to track down their friends and family members in their spare time.[50] An emerging ecosystem of consumer electronics that demand users install always-on microphones in their homes that record and transmit the most sensitive, private moments to third-party contractors screening the recordings for accurate transcription.[51] Give Americans a choice together—up or down—on abuses like these, and they'll say no every time. But no citizen can make that choice on her own. We all have to live in the world Big Tech has created around us.

An earlier generation of Americans might have wondered how all this was compatible with self-government by the people. How was it possible to sustain the broad and independent working class necessary for republican government in such a stratified economy, one that treated the vast majority of citizens as objects of manipulation? Theodore Roosevelt had balked at the monopolies of his day that consolidated power and crowded out the common man, but the robber barons' power over everyday Americans was nothing in comparison to that wielded by Big Tech. But then Roosevelt, and the earlier republican tradition he represented, thought freedom was grounded in *independence*. Economic independence. Independent judgment. In the republican tradition, these things were vital. No person with a master, no man or woman in thrall to someone else or subject to manipulation, could be truly free. The very possibility was ruinous to self-government and the personal liberty it sustained. But here was Big Tech, ceaselessly cajoling and nudging and manipulating. Here was Big Tech, attempting to shape the behavior of its users. Here was Big Tech, advancing the interests of a technological, managerial elite, a new aristocracy. Though in reality, Big Tech was not proposing to create a new aristocracy in America so much as to reshape and extend the old one it had inherited. The robber barons of the last century had given the nation a corporate elite. Big Tech would entrench that elite for a new era, redefining it around information and data control. The new overclass, the people with the greatest opportunity and the most influence, would be the tech professionals and their allied financiers, corporations, and bureaucratic enablers. They would run the country.

And where did that leave everyone else, the broad American middle? It left them as consumers rather than citizens, as objects rather than agents; it left them to suffer the effects of Big Tech's power grab and to absorb the costs of the addiction economy Big Tech pioneered. And those costs, it turns out, were enormous.

CHAPTER 6

ANTI-SOCIAL MEDIA

Researchers began to notice it in the mid-2010s, a new social feature, a quirk, a tic in the body politic. Americans were having trouble concentrating. Growing numbers of individuals, especially children and teens, just couldn't seem to focus. They were acting odd—distracted—unable to complete tasks like homework or basic reading without needing to reach for that small, shiny portal to the internet, the smartphone, and see what the world was saying on social media. They were acting addicted.

A 2014 study of phone users in the UK found owners checking their smartphones 221 times a day.[1] That's once every 4.3 minutes.[2] The effect was not salutary. Researchers found smartphones taxed owners' attention and reduced their problem-solving capacity even when not at hand, even when not in use. So strong was the lure of those flashes and badges and alerts designed by Google, Apple, and Facebook that they radically changed even the off-line behavior of their users. Concluded one study: "[T]he mere presence of consumers' own smartphones may adversely affect cognitive functioning even when consumers are not consciously attending to them."[3] That is to say, "Even if a phone's out of sight in a bag, even if it's set to silent, even if it's powered off, its mere presence will reduce someone's working memory and problem-solving skills."[4]

But that was the barest preview of the sort of social and psychological havoc the Big Tech addiction economy was unleashing on the public. Having addicted Americans to its platforms and services, having mined citizens' personal data, having subjected users to endless manipulation, Big Tech now demanded Americans absorb the potential consequences: soaring rates of depression, among children and teens especially; a dramatic spike in youth suicide; and a tangible loss of meaningful human relationships, as people turned away from each other and to their phones. There were political costs, too, visible in the outrage culture that Big Tech cultivated and promoted; there was the assault on common feeling and sentiment; the loss of deliberation, of the calm and informed reason that was supposed to animate political discussions. Far from empowering everyday Americans, Big Tech was assaulting the habits and mores of democratic life.

■ ■ ■

The worst of it had to do with children.

By the mid-2010s, the data on child social media use and time spent online was piling up, and alarms bells began pealing. Researchers found children more distracted than ever. One study reported that older children and teens could manage a mere six minutes of studying before indulging the compulsive need to pick up their smartphones and reconnect with social media.[5]

Other studies found American teens abandoning that famous teenage pastime—sleeping—in order to, yes, spend more time online. Teens who spent three or more hours a day on electronic devices, one report concluded, were 28 percent more likely than their peers to be significantly sleep-deprived. Teens who visited social media sites daily were nearly 20 percent more likely to lose sleep.[6] On balance, "57 percent more teens were sleep-deprived in 2015 than in 1991."[7] Between 2012 and 2015, the number of teens who failed to get even seven hours of sleep surged by 22 percent, even as smartphone usage soared.[8]

Here was a sight to behold, a snapshot from the Age of Big Tech: kids and teenagers eagerly spending their waking hours ignoring their classmates, declining conversation with living beings (including their parents), and forfeiting sleep in order to stumble about the house and around school and out in public incommunicative, with nose pressed to phone. Smartphones had suddenly become an electronic appendage of the teenage body. Part of the reason for this curious behavior previously unobserved in the species *homo sapiens* was the addictive design of the social media platforms and the products that displayed them, that is, the phones. But another reason, a prime reason, was *fear*. To be precise, the fear of missing out.

The social scientists who write what is called "social comparison theory" tell us that "people have an innate drive to compare the self to others, often in an attempt to obtain an accurate self-evaluation."[9] Call it human nature or the thirst for social status; Jean-Jacques Rousseau famously called it *amour propre*, a passion for recognition. Whatever the label, this drive accounts for much of what the human creature does with his or her time. Now imagine this innate need for social affirmation exposed to the vagaries of social media.

In the hallowed environs of Facebook and Instagram, the casual person who comes to browse finds row upon row, click upon click, image upon image of . . . perfect people. Hopelessly attractive, with-it, well-tailored, well-adjusted, having-the-best-time-of-their-lives people. That's because, as the social scientists tell us, the most successful posters to social media tend to "filter" their content. That is to say, they intend to make themselves as attractive, as envy-provoking, as flauntingly perfect as possible. *Here I am in Kuala Lumpur, on a cash-sucking yet tasteful excursion! Here are my superbly well-manicured yet delightfully authentic children on their first day of school!* And so on. A Facebook visitor might initially pop online to check on friends, search for acquaintances, or get up to speed on the latest social happenings—but! Soon she is tempted, as she browses, to do what all humans do, to *compare* herself with others, in this case with images of perfection that no reasonable person could hope to emulate.

Which brings us to the fear of missing out. This, the social theorists say, is "the pervasive apprehension"—or, for some teenagers, the god-awful *terror*—"that others might be having rewarding experiences from which one is absent."[10] If one has spent more than a few seconds on social media, it becomes obvious that fear of missing out is social media's stock-in-trade, its inevitable by-product, its very nature. And the dominant social media platforms are designed to maximize it.

Beginning in 2009, as social media's race to gain our attention kicked off in earnest, Facebook added a new feature to its platform to permit users to express approval of other users' posts and images. They called it the "like." It was a public token of popularity, a way to reward others of whom one approved *and* a metric that could be used to assess how popular one really was oneself. (As with many Facebook features, it was hardly original: Twitter had gotten there first with "favorites" a few years before, and Instagram would soon follow suit.) Research thereafter found that passive, casual browsing on Facebook was linked to lower life satisfaction, lower self-esteem, and depression; social comparison on Instagram was correlated with poor body image and anxiety.

Across social network sites, more time browsing led to more social comparison, more self-criticism, more *fear*. The social media sites practically ran on it. And the strange thing was, the more one suffered the fear of missing out, the more time one spent on social media.[11] Psychologists found fear of missing out consistently related to greater and greater levels of social media use. Isolated, nervous, depressed individuals couldn't seem to get enough—they were addicted, as if to a narcotic. The more time on social media, the lower one's self-esteem, and the lower one's self-esteem, the more one felt the craving for social approval, which was available, or not, on social media.

The data on how social media addiction led to sleep deprivation, lower self-esteem, and social isolation was worrying enough. But the truly terrifying consequences had to do with teen depression and suicide. In a study published in 2019, the proportion of high school seniors who said they often felt lonely increased from 26 to 39 percent in only five years.[12] The same study found that eighth graders today meet up with their friends, on average, sixty-eight *fewer* times a year than teens growing up in the 1990s, with similar declines for older age cohorts.[13] In a similar vein, the Center for Collegiate Mental Health at Penn State University reported in 2019 that indicators of student depression, anxiety, and social isolation had surged over the preceding decade, while more traditional college struggles like academic stress and substance abuse had held constant or even declined.[14]

What changed over the decades? A lot, no doubt, but mainly social media. In the words of one researcher, the "effect of screen activities is unmistakable: The more time teens spend looking at screens, the more likely they are to report symptoms of depression. Eighth-graders who are heavy users of social media increase their risk of depression by 27 percent, while those who play sports, go to religious services, or even do homework more than the average teen cut their risk significantly."[15]

Young girls in particular showed alarming signs of social isolation and anxiety correlated with social media use. Forty-eight percent more teen and pre-teen girls reported feeling "left out" in 2015 than in 2010; only 27 percent more boys said the same.[16] And while boys' depressive symptoms rose by 21 percent between 2012 and 2015, no small increase, girls' signs of depression skyrocketed by 50 percent over the same time period. Not surprising, perhaps, given that girls use social media appreciably more than boys, and appear more vulnerable to the sort of vicious and personal criticism meted out on social media platforms.[17]

The pervasiveness of social media means kids can feel its crushing effects without even picking up a phone or logging onto a computer. Social media use by even a few children in a group can change the entire atmosphere of a school or an organization. It's what is called "the network effect." Social scientist Jonathan Haidt explains that "if social media is part of the reason for the rise in teen depression [and] anxiety that began around 2012 . . . the causal path need not run through individual users." Because of social media, a few kids "may become more cruel, fearful, superficial, gossipy, or appearance-obsessed, and this could make many students more depressed and anxious, even if they do not use social media, or use it only lightly."[18]

And then there is the worst of it, teen suicide. The era of Big Tech has coincided with an epidemic of young people committing suicide, now the second leading cause of death for Americans between the ages of ten and twenty-four, behind only unintentional injuries such as automobile accidents and overdoses. Before the 2010s, suicide by young people had stabilized and declined for decades.[19] Not any longer. According to the Centers for Disease Control, the suicide rate jumped 56 percent in the decade leading up to 2017.[20]

As Professor Jean M. Twenge notes, young women, once again, have "borne the brunt of the rise in depressive symptoms among today's teens.... The rise in suicide, too, is more pronounced among girls. Although the rate increased for both sexes, three times as many 12-to-14-year-old girls killed themselves in 2015 as in 2007, compared with twice as many boys."[21]

Researchers are typically quick to note that the association of increased social media and smartphone usage on the one hand and pathologies like teen depression and suicide on the other are correlations only. The causal relationships are still under investigation and unknown. But with every passing day, the link appears stronger and more menacing.

There is more. Instagram's recommendation engine has become a notorious accelerant for "pro-eating-disorder" content.[22] And the COVID-19 era of social media culture suggests far worse may be yet to come. That year of widespread desperation, 2020, was not coincidentally also a year of trend pieces by corporate liberalism's apologists at outlets like the *New York Times* celebrating a new frontier in youth social media engagement: user-generated sexual content, often produced by teenagers, on platforms like OnlyFans. "You'd have to babysit a lot of hours to make $250, which I can do in a few hours of online sex work," one nineteen-year-old told the

Times. "I know because I babysat for a long time. I hated it."[23] Facebook hasn't yet acquired OnlyFans, but social media's next big platform is helping it find content creators. "I actually had no idea OnlyFans existed until I was recommended to do it" on TikTok, one user told The Verge.[24]

Psychiatrists began the 2010s debating whether "internet addiction" should be designated as an official psychiatric disorder, given the growing neurological research suggesting time online changed a young person's neurological gray matter.[25] By the decade's end, the point seemed moot. Depression rates were soaring, alongside social anxiety, personal isolation, and suicide. Big Tech had delivered something new, no question. It had helped create a social climate suffused with fear, oppressed by constant, public, vicious criticism and name-calling. And the worst of the burden was falling on the country's young.

Woodrow Wilson and his fellow corporate liberals had portrayed self-development as a form of liberty, *the* form of liberty most suited to, most needed in, the modern era. And yet the advent of social media made painfully, brutally clear that the search for self-development, self-expression, and originality could be as much a burden as a relief. The task of forging one's own personhood, of creating from the raw materials of life a truly original and authentic self, imposed the heaviest of expectations, especially on the young. Who could do it? Who could forge a personhood that was truly unique—whatever that meant—without the aid of family and home, without the influence of place and history? Was it even possible? The sort of liberty the corporate liberals had promised in exchange for the political, social, and economic dominance of the technocratic elite was worse than inadequate; it was itself a shackle, a burden that compromised one's confidence and independence.

Those many researchers and social scientists who catalogued the building anxiety, the darkening view of life, the growing loneliness and alienation, the spreading mental illness all associated with social media use, particularly among young people—these observers, whether they knew it or not, were in fact cataloguing the outcomes of late corporate liberalism. The republican tradition had identified liberty with the power to participate in public life, to exercise influence and have a say, and to do so from a position of independence, without being controlled by anyone else. Corporate liberalism proceeded along a different route. Its solipsistic doctrine of liberty as private choice, as self-actualization, surrendered individuals to the control of the powerful and stood by as the average person's influence ebbed away.

The private-choice liberty of corporate liberalism was, of course, a version of the liberty Big Tech assiduously promoted to sell its products and justify its power. And the irony was thick. Big Tech's *social* media platforms, the things Mark Zuckerberg said would connect the world, were perhaps the most anti-social devices in American history: not connecting, but isolating; not uniting, but dividing. And the dysfunction Big Tech was inflicting on the country in the name of "openness" and "connection," in the name of liberty, wasn't merely *personal* dysfunction, caused by tech-driven social isolation; it was *political* dysfunction, caused by tech-driven echo chambers of alienation and extremism.

■ ■ ■

It's a basic premise of republican thinking, going at least as far back as Aristotle, that citizens in a free state must be able to reason together about their common needs and interests, to deliberate. This is how citizens guide and control their government, by deliberating about what's good for them in common. James Madison followed this line of reasoning in his design of what became our Constitution, with its distinct branches of government and mandated sharing of power between nation and states. His ambition was to stymie the influence of powerful classes by, among other things, dispersing political power broadly, all with the aim of promoting measured deliberation by the people and their representatives. That's what made a republic a republic, after all, everyday people doing the deliberating and the deciding, their interests and needs setting the tone, not the designs of the high and mighty.

Only Big Tech is the high and mighty, the very definition. And Big Tech has gained powerful control over how we communicate in America—to a degree that would have horrified the founders. Social discourse is now centered on Big Tech's platforms, and Big Tech has no interest in promoting deliberative debate or empowering the common man. Deliberative debate requires common sentiments and loyalties, a shared horizon of interests and purposes, all of which social media has undermined. For profit. And control.

From the moment a social media user wanders online, the tech giants relentlessly track and monitor her every twitch and move, her every click and view, all for purposes of categorizing her. This categorizing, this herding of users, is supposed to reflect user interests, but its principal purpose is to make it easier to sell users *stuff*. Express an interest in Second Amendment rights, or share interests with others who do? The platform's almighty algorithm takes note, and shortly suggests to you potential gun-themed "friends" (on Facebook) and posts (on Instagram) and videos (on YouTube).

The algorithm makes mistakes, of course—mistakes that reveal the constant tracking to which the platforms subject their users. One grieving mother discovered after a tragic miscarriage that the baby ads wouldn't stop coming. "My world is very dark right now, it feels very empty," she told HuffPost. "It's the hardest thing seeing pregnant people and babies and buggies and anything to do with twins." But she couldn't get the ads to stop. She tried clicking the "hide" button, telling Instagram she wanted to "see fewer posts like this," but the platform—that intelligent AI—just wouldn't listen. Empathy isn't easy to code. Eventually she began searching the word "miscarriage" over and over again, hoping that would make the point. "I just didn't know what else to do, I felt really helpless throughout the pregnancy and now I feel even more helpless."[26]

But when the inferences are right or when you express an open preference, the social media algorithms really go to work. They amplify that preference by feeding you more and more content on that same subject, saturating your News Feed, your Timeline, your Autoplay. It's digital herding, algorithm-driven sorting, ostensibly to give users more of "what they want," but in reality to make it easier for the Big Tech companies to—of course—profit off you through targeted advertising.

Remember when Mark Zuckerberg promised a future where Facebook's all-knowing algorithms would expose users "to a greater number of diverse perspectives"? That was merely liberal happy talk. In reality, Facebook algorithms don't promote "diversity" at all, not diversity of views or association. They promote sameness. They force users into groups of similar people with similar interests and ideas. And once they have performed this herding, the Big Tech platforms proceed to promote the loudest and most obnoxious voices. The platforms called this promoting user "engagement," because outrage, it seems, sells.

A 2017 study by researchers at New York University found that each moral and emotional word used in a tweet boosted its online reach by an average of 20 percent.[27] A Pew Research Center study the same year reported that Facebook posts expressing "indignant disagreement" garnered *double* the user attention of other posts.[28] The like button and the retweet, introduced by Facebook and Twitter respectively in 2009, helped this effort along. They were expressly designed to channel user approval and—more to the point—disapproval. They quickly became conveyor belts of outrage. The News Feed and the Timeline provided the platforms opportunity to dump increasingly sensational and outrageous content right before users' eyes. Click on this! React to that! Much of the "news" was nonsense, it turned out, the headlines deliberately misleading, because on the News Feed anything could count as news. And did. But for the Big Tech platforms' purposes, it didn't matter. People were online, for hours at a time, stoking outrage. Which was just what Big Tech wanted.

Google was perhaps the most brazen practitioner of engagement by outrage. A major *New York Times* investigative report in 2019 found the YouTube Autoplay algorithm (YouTube is owned by Google) was responsible for fully 70 percent of time that users spent on the YouTube platform.[29] Once a user logged on, YouTube would begin recommending videos and content based on the user's initial selections or search history. The thing was, the more time the user spent online, the more sensationalized the video recommendations became. In the words of the *Times* report, the algorithm "rewards provocative videos with exposure and advertising dollars" and "guides users down personalized paths meant to keep them glued to their screens."[30]

This was entirely by design. In 2015, researchers from Google Brain, the tech giant's artificial intelligence unit, "began rebuilding YouTube's recommendation system around neural networks, a type of A.I. that mimics the human brain."[31] Google executives had noticed that YouTube customers eventually grew tired of seeing the same sort of content over and over. They wanted to change the algorithm to broaden the types of media suggestions YouTube made to its users, not by exposing them to fundamentally different content, but by surfacing related content the user might not think of himself—and, critically, content that was sensational, angry, and outraged. That is what kept users paying attention. The Google Brain team called the new algorithm "Reinforce." One executive admitted in 2017 that "the new algorithm was capable of drawing users deeper into the platform by figuring out 'adjacent relationships' between videos that a human would never identify."[32] The new algorithm was "a long-term addiction machine." Another Google researcher boasted at a conference in 2019 that the algorithm was even capable of altering users' behavior.[33]

Google, it seemed, was willing to shove just about any kind of content toward users to keep their attention, no matter the dangers, no matter the harm. In 2019, the *Times* reported that YouTube was funneling videos of partially clothed children to pedophiles.[34] YouTube's algorithm identified otherwise innocent videos of children—like a home movie made and uploaded by a young child in which he might be fleetingly partly undressed—and collected those videos and recommended them to people who had viewed sexually themed content or who had viewed multiple videos of prepubescent children. Worse, some of the videos were linked to the kids' social media accounts. The *Times* reported that some pedophiles who watched these videos, courtesy of YouTube, went on to contact the children in the videos and tried to "groom" them "into posting more sexualized pictures or engaging in sexual activity and having it videotaped."[35]

Within hours of reading the *Times* report, I proposed legislation banning YouTube and other platforms from recommending videos that featured minors.[36] I proposed criminal penalties for any violations, and heavy fines as well, to make YouTube feel the pain. Shortly after I announced my legislation, YouTube said it would "voluntarily" suspend the algorithmic recommending of content with minors, at least for a time.

But what Google refused to acknowledge was that the exploitation of children was hardly an isolated incident. It was a feature, a natural outcome, of the business model the company had deliberately, fervently embraced: engagement by outrage. And Google was not about to give that up.

As the Big Tech platforms pushed ahead with their outrage-focused engagement strategy, the toxic mores of social media began to lap over into everyday life. In the past, back in the real world, at a PTA meeting or a church get-together, a real person might call for a break if the discussion got heated, or perhaps remind himself of his neighbor's better qualities if annoyance started to set in. Not online. Online discussion did not proceed face to face, *mano a mano*. Oftentimes, one had never actually met, as in laid eyes upon in the actual flesh, one's digital conversation partner. And this was a problem. Psychologists have noticed, no surprise, that the normal behaviors that check escalating outrage—empathy, recall of shared experiences, time to step away—become seriously attenuated when disputants don't meet in person.[37] And the more people used social media, the more outrage performance gushed into the real world. It was the network effect, again. As outrage became the norm on the social platforms, researchers found that heavy social media users were taking their outrage with them into the workplace, the neighborhood, the church—in short, to those actual communities made up of actual people that had once been havens from the outrage-by-algorithm of online culture but were now increasingly subject to its contagion.[38] Recall the Google scientist's boast that algorithms could alter users' behavior.[39] Researchers found they increasingly were.

For democracy, for the republic of the common person, it all added up to trouble. Shuttling users into affinity groups by algorithm made terrific sense from an advertising perspective, but did nothing to promote the sort of real give-and-take that sustains the life of real communities. In fact, by encouraging individuals to spend more, and more, and more time online, social media helped accelerate the decline of actual associations where people used to go in times past to meet one another and forge relationships. It was there, in those places, that Americans acquired the shared experiences and sense of purpose that underwrote shared deliberation. The social media outrage factory was the very opposite of citizens reasoning together, Madisonian style, and the steadily growing role of the digital platforms in public discussion meant the steadily declining practice of actual discussion, of any kind.

If the republic depended on the views of the common person prevailing, on the ability of everyday people to deliberate together and achieve their common interests, social media was a republican nightmare. It divided the public, undermined a sense of shared fate, and stoked perpetual anger. And here again, Big Tech was bringing to fulfillment the logic of corporate liberalism.

Corporate liberalism's vision of liberty as private, personal choice placed almost no weight on deliberation or shared-in-common anything. This notion of liberty was deliberately atomizing *as a matter of principle*. It was meant to elevate the individual and diminish the importance of family, neighborhood, and church; it explained why these institutions' decline could safely be ignored—even celebrated. Corporate liberalism taught that there was no need to cultivate the habits of deliberation that made democracy work or to protect the communities where such deliberation occurred, no need to see personal freedom as linked to participation in democratic self-government. Instead, all that mattered was the celebration of individual choice.

Across the decades, this prevailing view had worked its influence. Both Right and Left now looked on liberty as something conferred rather than practiced, something that could coexist—as market choice, for conservatives; as expressive rights and social welfare, for progressives—with concentrated power, Big Tech being Exhibit A. And now Big Tech helped accelerate corporate liberalism's progress with predictable, though largely unpredicted, results: deepening cultural and political divisions; declining standards of deliberative debate; and increasing outrage, distrust, and fear. An old-fashioned republican would have called it a systematic assault on the public's virtue, on its independence and strength. But for Big Tech, it was opportunity.

As the power of the common person declined, the power of the Big Tech overclass multiplied: power over attention, over time, over users' judgment, and soon power over their speech. For speech was the next frontier. To achieve lasting social transformation, the Big Tech barons wanted to control what citizens read, to control their news and their reactions. To put it another way, the Big Tech barons wanted to become the censors of the nation.

CHAPTER 7

THE CENSORS

Less than three weeks before the 2020 presidential election, on October 17 to be exact, I was contacted by a whistleblower at Facebook—an employee who had worked on what the tech platforms call "content moderation," which means censorship, and wanted to report what he knew, which was plenty.

The timing was noteworthy. Only three days earlier, Facebook and Twitter had plunged into the middle of the presidential campaign by actively censoring a major *New York Post* investigative report detailing Hunter Biden's business dealings in Ukraine, including the potential involvement of his father, presidential candidate Joe Biden.[1] Within hours of the story's publication, Facebook announced it would "reduce distribution" of the report over its platform, meaning that it would effectively prevent users from sharing the story or, in some cases, from seeing it altogether.[2] Twitter went further. That platform stopped users from retweeting or linking to the story, or even sending private messages transmitting it. The platform locked the accounts of many users who tried, including the account of the *New York Post*, the oldest daily newspaper in America, founded by Alexander Hamilton.[3] Twitter would keep the *Post* locked out for sixteen days.[4] Both Facebook and Twitter loudly claimed as justification concern over possible "hacked" material or foreign disinformation in the *Post*'s reporting, though there would never be evidence of either.[5] Indeed, the director of national intelligence confirmed publicly a few days later that American intelligence agencies assessed the materials cited in the *Post* report not to be foreign disinformation and to be, indeed, apparently authentic.[6] By December, federal prosecutors would confirm that Hunter Biden was under criminal investigation for wire fraud and tax crimes associated with his overseas business dealings. Facebook and Twitter, however, refused to answer questions about how they had reached the decision to censor the *Post* story so quickly, and seemingly in tandem. And executives from the two companies steadfastly refused to say whether they had censored the report at the behest of the Biden presidential campaign.

In the midst of this uproar, an individual who went by the name of Mike Gilgan made contact with my office. It was a pseudonym. Like many whistleblowers, he was eager to keep his true identity anonymous, and understandably. He had only recently left Facebook; he feared that if his identity were revealed, executives there would try to prevent him from working in the tech sector ever again.

When he contacted us, he offered to share what he knew about Facebook's censorship and privacy practices. I was interested but proceeded with caution. My office first worked to verify "Mike Gilgan's" credibility. On October 27, several of my staff members spoke to him at some length—over a secure phone line, at Gilgan's request. On October 30, he agreed to meet with a member of my team in person.

The details he revealed were based on his personal knowledge from his time at Facebook. He produced documentary evidence to back them up. And it was all startling. Facebook was deep in the censorship business, Gilgan confirmed, and the company's ability to track and monitor what its users were saying and doing was beyond anything yet publicly disclosed. There was more. Facebook didn't censor by itself. No, the Big Tech platforms *coordinated* their censorship, which my team thought might help explain the simultaneous actions of Facebook and Twitter on the *New York Post* story.

And in a way, it made perfect sense. Big Tech was more than a group of monopolies; it was a *movement*, just as the corporatists of the Gilded Age had represented a movement to change American life. The modern-day corporatists, Big Tech, had similar ambitions. As Zuckerberg had said, Facebook "was built to accomplish a social mission," and together the tech barons were using their power over news, information, and speech to help bring their social vision into reality. Their aim was to build a more "open," "connected," "global" America, the kind Mark Zuckerberg had written about in his first letter to shareholders, a society that reflected the "progressive" outlook of the twenty-first-century professional class. And to realize that vision, to change society, the tech platforms had to change the manners and morals of the people *in* society. Which is just what they were aiming to do.

■ ■ ■

Mike Gilgan knew Facebook's censorship practices. He had seen them in action. He could rattle off the deliberately prosaic names the company assigned its various censorship teams: there was the "Integrity Team," the "Hate Speech Engineering Team," and the "Community Well-Being Team." And he knew what these teams were up to. When he spoke to us, Gilgan still had access to some internal Facebook platforms and materials, which was one of the reasons we assessed him to be credible. And it turns out there was quite a lot of talk about censorship at Facebook.

Facebook didn't make censorship decisions at random, not according to Gilgan. Nor did the company simply leave them to the whims of algorithms. Real, living humans at Facebook made scores of censorship decisions, including the most sensitive ones, working across the company's various content moderation teams with a tool called Tasks.

Tasks was an internal Facebook platform built to coordinate employees' projects at the company. Employees from all divisions used it, including, Gilgan told us, Mark Zuckerberg. Items listed on the Tasks platform were open to employees of the company. Employees could enter new items on the platform, a sort of to-do list, and initiate internal Facebook discussion groups. For example, Gilgan said, a software engineer might enter a "task" saying "I need to build a new widget, like a play or a pause button," and other employees could help or comment. Tasks could be broken down into main items and various sub-items. The Tasks tool allowed the requesting individual to list a title, description, and comment thread. Gilgan explained that Facebook employees could "like" comments within the task and tag coworkers to keep them updated on a task's progress.

Facebook's censorship teams used Tasks. According to Gilgan, it was where many censorship decisions were ultimately made. A censorship team might open a new task with a subject such as "ban this URL" and start a discussion thread where censorship team members could loop in their bosses to hash out the issue. Sometimes the censorship tasks mentioned suppressing particular individuals. Based on what Gilgan told us, many of the sites and individuals targeted by Facebook censors appeared to be conservatives or rightward-leaning. He said that Facebook censors consulted leftist sources in deciding who and what to censor. Those sources included the Southern Poverty Law Center, a left-wing, anti-religious group that has repeatedly attacked Christian organizations and individuals as "racist" or "bigoted" and has itself recently been in the news for the misdeeds of its founder.[7]

As an example of the sort of leftist, anti-conservative bias that prevails at Facebook, Gilgan revealed screenshots of Antifa groups organizing on a Facebook internal platform called Workplace. One employee proudly stated that he burns the American flag every year on the Fourth of July. Gilgan also turned over the name of an individual who he knew had been fired for complaining about the Antifa comments in 2019. Facebook's internal platforms were dominated by far-left content, Gilgan said.

But perhaps the biggest news about censorship was what Gilgan told us about who else Facebook consults when it comes to banning sites and users: Twitter. And Google. On a regular basis. The biggest Big Tech social platforms were teaming up.

Gilgan revealed that Facebook censorship team members frequently spoke to their counterparts at Twitter and Google and coordinated their censorship efforts. The Tasks platform told the tale. According to Gilgan, numerous censorship entries on Tasks referenced Google and Twitter domain names, as well as particular phrases, words, URLs, or individuals the three platforms were jointly considering suppressing. Facebook censors used the Tasks platform to log the suggestions and tips of their Google and Twitter counterparts. As an example, Gilgan specifically recalled a lengthy thread openly referencing contacts at Twitter, discussing a proposal to suppress multiple conservative commentators. Other threads referenced the Southern Poverty Law Center. Gilgan showed us screenshots of the Tasks platform with repeated entries under the label "election integrity."

There was more. Tasks was not the only tool Facebook used for monitoring its users' speech. Facebook had developed a powerful tracking platform to spy on customers' speech and activity. It was called Centra. Gilgan described Centra as a supercharged version of Messenger, Facebook's text messaging app, that could both track and aggregate any Facebook user's activity pattern across the entire internet—and across all the user's devices. To be clear, it wasn't just that Facebook could monitor users' activity on Facebook pages and related sites. Centra gave Facebook the power to follow its users practically wherever they went, to any site that had a Facebook button or connection or plug-in. The Centra tool contained a category named "SUMA"—Same User, Multiple Accounts. This allowed Facebook's algorithms to detect if a user was trying to evade recognition by logging in pseudonymously. Centra could also track the user's messages and his message recipients.

Gilgan showed us a screenshot of Centra in action, monitoring an individual whose first name was Younis (I've omitted his last name). His status was recorded as "active," his birthday as October 3, 1994. His age was noted (25 at the time), as well as the precise time and date of his last login. The Centra platform recorded 21 linked Facebook accounts, one linked Instagram account, 2,856 message recipients, and 3,177 message threads. It recorded the number of other Facebook profiles Younis had visited, his videos, his commented posts (4,159), his administrative records, and his record of "harmful media" (26), among other things. It was an extraordinary mine of information, a surveillance hub run by Facebook.

Inside the company, according to Gilgan, employees talked frequently about the kind of content moderation the company was performing using Centra. Centra could produce statistical analyses of messaging habits, including scatterplots. Gilgan worried the platform was in and of itself a privacy violation. *Why should employees be able to see a user's private messages to his friends or family or spouse?* he wondered. And here was the kicker: there was no real oversight.

Facebook policies formally required an audit anytime someone at Facebook accessed a user's private messages or personally identifiable data, according to Gilgan. But Gilgan said no one he knew had ever been audited, whether in connection with Centra or more generally. Indeed, he didn't believe audits happened at all. Facebook ostensibly had a security mechanism in place that cut off access to user data after ninety days of inactivity, Gilgan said. But one of the first things he did at Facebook was design a tool to reconstruct user data and activity patterns even after the cutoff. The truth was, Facebook was exceptionally lax, even cavalier, about user privacy. Centra was a glaring case in point. A Facebook employee with access to Centra could track individuals anywhere, see every device ever associated with their Facebook accounts and every social media account ever connected to their personal devices. And all this without meaningful restraints or controls.

Gilgan's revelations were shocking. They disclosed a company rife with political bias and arrogant with power. Facebook mouthed platitudes about user privacy and choice; company executives disclaimed any political manipulation or unequal treatment; but the truth was clearly otherwise. Facebook had a political agenda, or more precisely, a social agenda, and it was determined to use its power to achieve it. User privacy and data security were treated as niceties to be rehearsed in public and then ignored.

The information Gilgan provided was timely not only for the light it shed on the *New York Post* controversy and for what it suggested about Facebook, Twitter, and Google's apparently coordinated censorship campaigns. It came just in time for a public hearing before the Senate Judiciary Committee featuring none other than Mark Zuckerberg.

Zuckerberg and Jack Dorsey, Twitter's CEO, had agreed to appear before the judiciary committee after the *New York Post* furor reached a fever pitch, and then only on pain of subpoena. Getting the committee to vote on the subpoenas had been a feat in itself. The Democrats on the committee had no interest in speaking to Zuckerberg or Dorsey on this topic, not given the details of the *Post* story involving the Bidens and how such revelations might be important to undecided voters. Republicans on the judiciary committee were also reticent. Some Senate Republicans have a warm relationship with Big Tech; some take tech money. Others are influenced by the cacophony of pro-tech voices in D.C. think tanks and lobbyist shops, influence for which Big Tech has paid handsomely. Still others object on principle to efforts to break up concentrated corporate power. In any event, when I first demanded the Senate Judiciary Committee subpoena Zuckerberg and Dorsey before the election, I couldn't find many supporters. Some Republican senators were comfortable subpoenaing Dorsey. Few wanted to include Zuckerberg. And a number wanted no subpoenas at all. After my vocal calls for a hearing, I was approached on the Senate floor by one Republican colleague who asked me to stand down and let the issue drop. My staff was lobbied intently by others. I refused.

Finally, under public pressure and with the November election looming, the committee agreed to subpoena the two tech titans. The vote carried on October 22, on strictly party lines; no Democrat voted in support, but every Republican voted yes, a few through clenched teeth. Zuckerberg and Dorsey ultimately agreed to appear without the subpoena, after the election.

So it was that on November 17, 2020, I again sat opposite Mark Zuckerberg, this time via a satellite connection, and put to him the star-tling questions raised by "Mike Gilgan." I asked if Facebook coordinated censorship decisions with Twitter and Google. Zuckerberg prevaricated. "Senator, let me be clear about this. We—we do coordinate on—and share signals on security-related topics."[8] "Security-related topics" was a phrase capacious enough to include any manner of contacts, as Zuck-erberg surely knew. I pressed. On content moderation, censorship, did Facebook coordinate with the other Big Tech giants? Zuckerberg initially denied it—"Senator, we do not coordinate," he said—but then quickly added that Facebook censorship team members *might* speak with their counterparts at Google and Twitter. "Senator, I'm not aware of anything specific, but I—I think it would be probably pretty normal for people to talk to their—their peers and colleagues in the industry," he said.[9]

I was intrigued by this half admission. "It would be normal, but you don't do it?" I asked.

"No, I—I—I'm—I'm saying that I—I'm—I'm not aware of any par-ticular conversation, but I would expect that some level of—of communi-cation probably happened," Zuckerberg said, fumbling for his words.

I asked if Facebook would prove it. Would Zuckerberg release the records from the Tasks platform detailing any contacts with Twitter or Google on censorship questions? Zuckerberg stammered. "Senator, I—I think it would be better to—to follow up once I've had a chance to discuss with my team. . . ."[10] Let me get back to you, he said. In other words, no.

And then we came to Centra. Zuckerberg was clearly surprised by my mention of the tracking platform, as Gilgan had predicted he would be. I asked whether he knew of Centra. Appearing slightly flummoxed, Zuckerberg initially said he knew of no such platform. "Senator, I'm not aware of any tool with that name."[11] I showed him the picture of the Centra platform Mike Gilgan had shared with me, the one with all the information about Younis and his activity online. Seeing that, Zucker-berg shifted his story. "I'm sure that we have tools that help us with our platform and community integrity work," he said, meaning censorship, "but I—I am not familiar with that name."[12] I was beginning to notice that the longer I talked with Zuckerberg, the dimmer his memory grew. I pushed. Do you have this tool, I asked, or are you denying it exists at all? Will you tell us whether it has been used to track American citizens on American soil? Now Zuckerberg was in full damage control. "Senator, I—I'm saying that I'm not familiar with—and that I'd be happy to follow up and—and get you and your team the information that—that you would like on this. But I—I'm limited what I can—what I'm familiar with and can share today."[13] Not one hour later, while Zuckerberg was still before the committee, Facebook headquarters issued a statement confirming that Centra *did* exist.[14] But the company refused to answer whether it used the platform to track Americans in the domestic United States, or provide any further details.

I tried again a week later with written questions "for the record," as they are called, follow-up questions Senate committees issue to witnesses in writing after a hearing. I directed my questions to both Zuckerberg and Dorsey, asking for details on Tasks, on Centra, on coordinated censorship between the companies and efforts to track Americans' speech. Instead they responded with boilerplate language about content moderation.

■ ■ ■

Mike Gilgan's revelations confirmed a pattern. Big Tech censors now had the power to determine what information ordinary Americans had access to and what information would be directed to them. They were determined to enforce the social, cultural, and political biases of their class: the high-earning, coastally enclaved, liberal-corporatist class, firmly committed to the free flow of labor and capital across borders and to the profit motive, or at least to *their* profits, which were plentiful.

In the spring of 2016, former Facebook contract workers admitted to reporters that they "routinely suppressed news stories of interest to conservative readers from the social media network's influential 'trend-ing' news section."[15] The trending box was prime advertising real estate, given the number of eyes it drew. It was reserved for news that was viral, that no reader wanted to miss—unless it promoted conservative ideas.

Facebook contractors working on trending news, internally called "news curators," said they intervened to squelch stories on topics ranging from Obama-era IRS targeting of conservatives to campaign news from presidential candidate Mitt Romney. The "curators" reviewed and man-aged the list of trending topics as generated by a Facebook algorithm. Their job was to dash off headlines and summaries for topics the algo-rithm identified as hot *and* to block stories that didn't fit their prejudices. "Depending on who was on shift, things would be blacklisted or trend-ing," one former curator told reporters. "It was absolutely bias," said another. "We were doing it subjectively. It just depends on who the curator is and what time of day it is."[16]

In addition to nixing news supportive of or of interest to conserva-tives, the curators intervened against conservative websites. "Every once in awhile a Red State or conservative news source would have a story," said one former curator. "But we would have to go and find the same story from a more neutral outlet that wasn't as biased"—*biased* meaning conservative, in this lexicon, while progressive outlets were deemed mainstream and reliable.[17]

Curators occasionally helped the algorithm along in other ways, by inserting topics they thought the public *should* care about. The curating team called it "injection." "We were told that if we saw something, a news story that was on the front page of these ten sites, like CNN, the *New York Times*, and BBC, then we could inject the topic," one former curator reported. The main focuses of these stories were foreign policy issues or topics deemed particularly important to management, like the Black Lives Matter movement. "Facebook got a lot of pressure about not having a trending topic for Black Lives Matter," according to a former curator. "They"—meaning management—"realized it was a problem, and they boosted it in the ordering. They gave it preference over other topics." Indeed, on more than once occasion, a topic "injected" into the trending news module went on to become the top trending news item on Facebook, a real-time demonstration of the platform's power to influence readers and the news.[18]

None of this was remotely surprising given the background of the curators: according to reports, they were a set of young journalists educated largely at elite universities.[19] They were merely imposing the cultural preferences of their social class—and of the rest of Big Tech. What was surprising was Facebook's inability to be honest about what it was doing. Mark Zuckerberg boldly declared he wanted Facebook to be "the primary news experience people have,"[20] a place for real news, real information. Facebook also insisted that the trending news module merely listed "topics that have recently become popular on Facebook,"[21] even though Facebook took an editorial interest in deciding what was and should be popular.

Partly in response to the controversy over its curators, Facebook eventually abandoned the trending news module, but by no means did it abandon its broader agenda of pushing an ideological line. If anything, the 2016 election seemed to mark a watershed in this regard. In the weeks immediately following Trump's victory, Zuckerberg vowed to crack down on "fake news" across social media.[22] The implication was that "fake news" had helped propel Donald Trump to the presidency. The 2016 election results created a fierce urgency at Facebook and the Big Tech platforms. The companies would root out "fake news" and help better educate the populace.

In 2018, Zuckerberg announced Facebook would start explicitly doing what its curator team had tried to accomplish behind closed doors, this time by altering its algorithms to rank news organizations according to "trust" and to suppress stories from those outlets not deemed worthy.[23] Zuckerberg sold the change as content-neutral, having nothing to do with a given news site's political provenance. But Facebook executive Campbell Brown adjusted this pronouncement a short time later by explaining Facebook would indeed "have a point of view" and lean into "quality news."[24] And "quality" here meant the liberal establishment media. That same year, the nonpartisan social analytics company News-Whip reported that Facebook's new algorithm yielded big boosts for legacy outlets like CNN and NBC, while generating sharp readership declines for smaller, politically focused sites.[25] The tech website The Outline issued its own report in the spring of 2018, finding that "conservative and right-wing publishers (such as Breitbart, Fox News, and Gateway Pundit) were hit the hardest in the weeks following the announcement, with Facebook engagement totals . . . dropping as much as 55 percent for some." Meanwhile, "the engagement numbers of most predominantly liberal publishers remained unaffected."[26]

■ ■ ■

Google embraced the responsibilities of the censor with equal fervor. The 2016 election had been as radicalizing for Google as it had been for Facebook. In the aftermath of Donald Trump's election that year, Google employees were so distraught that the management team convened a corporate-wide sympathy session. Google cofounder Sergey Brin acknowledged that "most people here are pretty upset and pretty sad" with the outcome, and assured his employees that "as an immigrant and a refugee, I certainly find this election deeply offensive, and I know many of you do too."[27] Not to be outdone, Google vice president Kent Walker observed that "fear, not just in the United States but around the world, is fueling concerns, xenophobia, [and] hatred."[28]

One can understand the disappointment, given the effort Google had already made to stop Trump's election. Facebook had its News Feed; Google had Search. And Search could alter election outcomes. Research psychologist Robert Epstein began studying what he termed the "search engine manipulation effect" back in 2014. It had to do with the placement of news articles and other links returned to users in a Google Search query. Because Google Search had become so efficient (the algorithms again) and the site itself so widely used, Google's customers had come to expect that the higher an item appeared on the list of search results, the more relevant and trustworthy that item must be.[29] Epstein found as early as 2014 that he could alter the choice of undecided voters in an election by perhaps more than 12 percent simply by manipulating the order of the search results—a swing that could determine a close contest.[30]

That was all hypothetical. Then came the 2016 presidential election. Epstein, a liberal Democrat, exhaustively studied Google's Search responses for months leading up to Election Day, conducting more than 13,000 election-related searches on 3 different search engines with changing groups of voters. What he found was a pronounced search bias on Google in favor of Democratic presidential candidate Hillary Clinton. According to Epstein, the "Google search results—which dominate search in the U.S. and worldwide—were significantly biased in favor of [former] Secretary [of State] Clinton in all 10 positions on the first page of search results in both blue states and red states."[31] What did it mean? Professor Epstein estimated that Google's secret, proprietary, almighty algorithm likely nudged 2.6 *million* undecided voters toward Hillary Clinton.[32]

It happened again in 2018. In the weeks leading up to the midterm elections, Epstein determined that bias in Google's search results "may have shifted upwards of 78.2 million votes" toward Democratic Party candidates.[33] The evidence, Epstein concluded, showed "strong political bias."[34]

And Search wasn't Google's only means of "educating" the electorate. As every Google user knows, the platform will helpfully suggest search terms to the user the moment one begins to type a query into the Google Search box. Epstein found that this feature, called "autocomplete," also had a remarkable nudging effect on undecided or relatively uninformed voters. Remarkable meant this: autocomplete suggestions could convert an even 50/50 split among unaligned voters to a 90/10 landslide, all without users' knowledge.[35] And in the 2016 and 2018 elections, Google's autocomplete feature routinely suggested queries to voters favoring the more liberal candidate. In Epstein's analysis, "In the months leading up to the 2016 presidential election in the U.S., it was difficult to get Google to show you negative search suggestions for

Hillary Clinton, even though negative search terms were predominant for Clinton on Google."[36] By contrast, four of the first five autocomplete suggestions for Donald Trump in October 2017 were negative.[37] Epstein's bottom-line conclusion was startling. "Google," he said, "has likely been determining the outcomes of upwards of 25 percent of the national elections in the world since at least 2015."[38] Now *that* was power.

And Google, like Facebook, was committed to using this power appropriately, responsibly, for the public's benefit and moral uplift— which happened to coincide with Big Tech's political preferences. To give users "greater context" in understanding the news that Google was funneling to them, the company experimented in 2017 with "fact checks" at the top of its search results page. The fact checks were written by *respected* outside groups, which predictably meant left-wing advocacy groups like Snopes and Climate Feedback.[39] The fact-check feature was so obviously biased that Google yanked it barely a year later.[40]

Google had another subtler but equally powerful lever of influence: its advertising platform. Its various advertising networks—AdSense, AdMob, Admeld, DoubleClick—permitted online publishers, like news outlets and other websites, to sell space on their sites to advertisers. For online publishers, it was a major revenue stream, *the* revenue stream, practically the only game in town. To be excluded from it was a financial death knell, especially for a small news site. In the spring of 2020, Google began threatening conservative-leaning websites with exclusion from the advertising platform unless they made various concessions, including suspending their comments section and revising their news stories. One prominent target was The Federalist, a conservative site frequently critical of Google. After NBC News complained about The Federalist's reporting, Google threatened to bar The Federalist from its advertising network. Since that might look like politically motivated censorship, Google quickly shifted to The Federalist's comments section, saying the site wasn't doing enough to moderate it and delete objectionable comments—a duty, incidentally, Google insisted was impracticable for its own services, such as YouTube. The Federalist ultimately appeased

Google by eliminating its comments section, but Google's threat was plain. It had the power to defund conservative websites.[41]

■ ■ ■

Then there was Big Tech's control over the content of the news, over journalism itself. Big Tech had become the biggest news publisher in America.

In the spring of 2020, a string of news sites and media companies announced deep job cuts. Nancy Dubuc, CEO at one of the worst hit, Vice Media, pointed the finger squarely at Big Tech. "Big Tech," she said, poses "a great threat to journalism."[42] Big Tech was a bigger problem than pandemics or business cycles or changing consumer habits, because in a sense Big Tech *determined* consumer habits and *controlled* the business cycle for news sites. News sites are dependent on advertising revenue, and by 2020 more than 60 percent of all digital advertising revenue went to just three sources: Facebook, Google, and Amazon.[43]

After holding steady for decades, ad spending on print journalism plunged in the 2010s, reflecting a similarly precipitous drop in print readership.[44] Digital ad spending, by contrast, boomed.[45] People were still reading, still consuming news. But they were reading it in a different place, not on folded sheafs of paper delivered to the driveway each morning, but by the cold blue light of the tablet and smartphone. *That* was the twenty-first century.

And the big news battle of the century was, *where* online would Americans read their news? Would it be on the respective websites of established news publishers? Or on the platforms where more and more Americans spent more and more of their time, Facebook and Google and Apple? The race for readership and the flow of advertiser dollars was on, publishers versus Big Tech, and by the end of the 2010s, Big Tech was winning. Big-time.

As it turns out, readers weren't fans of scouring the recesses of the internet looking for news. They wanted to find it in one or two places, predictable places where they already spent time, the digital equivalent of the morning newspaper. And Big Tech knew just how to deliver it to them. In 2006, Facebook added a feature called News Feed, a centralized stream on users' home pages containing updates from Facebook friends and, from time to time, actual news.[46] The News Feed was, of course, mainly an effort at keeping users engaged and winning their attention, but over time it became, for many Facebook users, a significant source of news. One survey from the Pew Research Center in 2018 showed that fully 43 percent of Americans got their news from Facebook, making the company, in the words of the study, "far and away the site Americans most commonly use for news."[47] And that meant Facebook became a major recipient of news advertising dollars.

Google took a different approach, emphasizing its signature product, Google Search. Or as Google liked to call it by the 2010s, Universal Search, because it was meant to encompass *everything,* every possible search need in the world, every query from sales to weather to, yes, news. When a user typed a word or phrase in the Google Search bar, the company's proprietary algorithms returned pages of hyperlinks, allegedly ranked according to relevance. But when a user typed in a term the algorithm identified as having news content, Google did something more: it presented the user with links to stories from news sites—*and* a "Top Stories" carousel at the head of the page, a box that included articles, videos, and live blogs displayed horizontally and with images. And who decided what stories appeared in the Top Stories carousel? Why, the Google algorithm, of course.[48]

Users loved it. One recent and comprehensive report from Australia found that up to 14 percent of user search queries were related to news and thereby triggered the appearance of the Top Stories carousel.[49] Google was not just a search engine. In the twenty-first century, it was a newspaper, a television station, and a radio station all in one. Google *was* news. And the numbers reflected it: news advertising dollars were flowing to Google and Facebook in ever greater amounts. The losers were the legacy publishers, the traditional news sites that became supplicants to Google. These sites needed Big Tech for referrals because readers increasingly came to traditional news outlets only *after* finding a story or video linked on Google or Facebook.[50] For all intents and purposes, in the Tech Age, the Big Tech platforms were the biggest news publishers on the planet.

This new dispensation in news meant good money, very good money—for Big Tech. By one estimate, in 2018 Google raked in $4.7 billion from news content alone, about as much as all the other news organizations in the country put together earned from digital advertising.[51] And unlike the news sites, Google and Facebook paid practically nothing for content; they merely circulated it, highlighted it—and hit a commercial jackpot.

Journalists were less than enthralled. As Nancy Dubuc of Vice put it, "[A]fter many years of this, the squeeze is becoming a chokehold. Platforms are not just taking a larger slice of the pie, but almost the whole pie."[52] The layoffs in early 2020 were only the latest in a long line. Between 1990 and 2016, the newspaper industry shed some 30,000 jobs, while "news media ad revenue plunged by $30 billion between 2006 and 2017."[53]

It didn't have to be this way. In the early days of the digital "revolution," the tech platforms needed the traditional publishers—they needed publishers' content to make their aggregation services worthwhile and profitable. And the publishers might have imposed more favorable terms on their relationship. Google had no natural right, after all, to trawl the publishers' sites for free to build out its own search index. Google just did it. But by the time publishers realized what had happened, how they had been outmaneuvered, it was too late; denying Google and Facebook access to their content would have been business suicide, given the power of Big Tech to direct readers' attention.

Big Tech became not only a news distributor, but a news creator—of headlines, format, topics, and content. One former news executive recalled meetings with Google, Facebook, and the Facebook-owned Instagram at which the tech wizards instructed their unprofitable journalistic counterparts how to optimize their reportage for the platforms' algorithms. Because now, the almighty algorithm was everything. It was the algorithms that determined what appeared in the News Feed, what got sent to the Google "Top Stories" box, what was deemed "trending" or breaking . . . or not. It was these algorithms that now held the future of journalism in the balance. The lowly producers of the news—the actual journalists, and their editors and publishers—now had to listen, and obey, their tech masters.

"Pivot to video! Make Snap stories, but only if you prove to us you've hired a dedicated team! Change the way you write headlines! Hand over subscription signups to us!" barked the platform experts.[54] Big Tech and the news publishers weren't competing any longer; Big Tech now controlled the whole game. For years Google had suggested, in the tone of a mob enforcer suggesting a protection fee, that publishers adopt a "First Click Free" policy for users lest their search ranking fall off a cliff. Then came a new demand: that news sites publish their stories in the digital format Google dictated, a format that hosted content on Google's servers to maximize ease of viewing on Google Search. This same digital formatting made it more difficult for news sites to advertise within their own stories and minimized publisher data collection, while maximizing it for Google.[55]

Facebook made its own demands. Beginning in the summer of 2015, Facebook famously ordered news organizations to replace written stories with video segments because videos performed better on Facebook platforms, were shared more often, and spread more rapidly. Or so Facebook claimed. Desperate news divisions pliantly obeyed, cutting hundreds of reporters in favor of video editors and graphic designers, only to learn a year or two later that Facebook had invented its video "data" out of thin air, overstating the time users spent watching video segments by as much as 900 percent.[56]

Before the fraud was exposed, astute observers recognized that the pivot to Facebook-hosted video content wasn't a mere marketing annoyance. It was, in the words of The Awl's John Herrman, Facebook's "first major attempt to requisition the media that it has up until this point partnered with. . . . All the things we link to on Facebook now, Facebook could conceivably host. . . . [T]he headlines that were once designed to convince you to click and leave Facebook for a few seconds will now be responsible only for convincing you to look at the thing immediately below (if there are traditional headlines at all)." Once the Facebook hamster wheel was fully constructed, there would be no off-loading of users to third-party websites. The publishers, Herrman noted, would now need to become Facebook "creators" if they wanted Facebook's audience.[57]

Apple was supposed to be different from the other predatory tech giants. Steve Jobs was a man of culture. "I don't want to see us descend into a nation of bloggers," he lamented to journalists worried over their industry's future. And he had just the thing to save them. He called it the iPad. It would come with a built in App Store subscription feature. "Anything we can do to help the *New York Times*, *Washington Post*, *Wall Street Journal* and other news gathering organizations find new ways for expression so they can afford to get paid, so they can afford to keep their news gathering editorial operations intact, I'm all for," Jobs said.[58]

But Jobs had a penchant for exaggeration. By "anything we can do," he meant anything that cut Apple in—forever—as the toll-master of subscription revenues. News apps published through Apple's "newsstand" would be subject to Apple's collection of a 30 percent cut on subscription revenues, along with all the data on the publications' App Store customers. It was a win-win . . . for Apple and Apple.[59]

And 30 percent was just a start. Jobs's successor, Tim Cook, had a reputation as a numbers guy. He decided that the 30 percent cut was leaving money on the table. So, in 2019, Apple developed a news aggregator of its own, Apple News+, a subscription-based service that promised to deliver curated news content from a rainbow of news media directly to subscribers for a small monthly fee, of which Apple would take . . . 50 percent.[60] Apple would not, of course, generate any of this content itself; that would be done by other people, the journalists. But Apple was doing them a favor (according to Apple). The company would guarantee journalists an audience, and take merely half the profit in return.

Jeff Bezos of Amazon, meanwhile, was not to be outdone. He knew a trend when he saw one. Bezos didn't control a general search engine. He didn't run his own social network. So the wealthiest man on planet earth made things simpler: he just bought the *Washington Post* outright.

The Big Tech platforms' power over advertising and sway over consumer attention now made them the biggest publishers in the history of the world. Their sudden, sprawling influence was difficult for the oldtimers to fathom, and in this case old-timer meant any journalist over thirty. What you wrote, what news outlet published it—none of that mattered anymore. The traditional status symbols were defunct. If a story wasn't on the News Feed, if it wasn't picked up by Google, if it wasn't blessed by the almighty algorithms, it practically didn't exist. And to get picked up by the News Feed and Google, the *content* of what journalists wrote changed as well.

To please the almighty algorithm, to get eyeballs and clicks, stories became shorter, more sensational, and more tinged with controversy. Wary journalists referred to pieces that met these all-important criteria, that pleased the algorithmic fates, as "clickbait." In the great Age of Tech, journalism *was* clickbait, and Big Tech controlled the clicks.

■ ■ ■

If corporate liberalism had dreamed of government by the experts, the woke capitalists of Big Tech were able to go them one better: now the biggest news publishers in the world could work in tandem with liberal-corporatists in government, in the business world, and in other establishment institutions to advance the cause of "progress." They would "educate" and "enlighten" the public, censor unhelpful opposing voices, and do it all out of sight, concealed behind algorithms and bland statements about "quality journalism."

Big Tech's progressive social agenda—pro-LGBT, pro-abortion, pro–Black Lives Matter—commended it to liberals who knew an ally when they saw one and who believed that the public badly needed "education" on these issues. Indeed, liberal politicians pressed Big Tech to do more: to "fact-check" conservative outlets and politicians, especially Donald Trump; to block conservative political ads; to police speech that transgressed progressive taboos. All of which Twitter and Google and YouTube and Instagram and Facebook dutifully did. When liberals expressed qualms about Big Tech's power, it was usually when tech bungled its information control (or censorship), as when Facebook permitted Russian bots to run a series of political advertisements during the 2016 election season. The problem, as the Left saw it, wasn't that Big Tech had too much power over information; it was that Big Tech sometimes *failed* to use it to advance the progressive agenda.

The Right, for its part, seemed unable to fathom the danger of censorship and control from capital. Big Tech was supposed to be a business success story, the result of free market ingenuity and freely made consumer choices. A century of corporate liberalism had done its work: much of the Right appeared incapable of conceiving any threat to liberty that was not a threat to consumer choice. (Leaving aside the inconvenient fact that it was largely Big Tech, not consumers, who were making the choices.) That Big Tech's growing power might undermine the average person's control over his personal data, his daily life, his access to information, his ability to exercise any real social influence and political authority . . . that seemed not to stir the Right in the least. Or not much of it.

And so on Big Tech went, the censors for a new generation, entrenching the social influence of the new corporate class. For at the end of the day, Big Tech was not the change agent its spokesmen liked to imagine. It was, in a truer sense, an advocate of continuity. Big Tech wanted the same sort of society the first corporate liberals wanted, a society managed by the professional elite. And the tech barons were determined that this elite would be led by them.

CHAPTER 8

NEW WORLD ORDER

It was not by accident that the corporate legislation enacted by Woodrow Wilson in the first years of his presidency, the "settlement" that pressed the antitrust issue to the sidelines, also included a major revision to the country's famous protective tariff. That tariff had been the centerpiece of the nation's manufacturing policy for more than half a century. It reflected a vision of what American life should be, a place where domestic industry would flourish and where workers could support themselves with their own hands. Wilson revised it sharply downward, and the corporate lobby cheered the change all the way. The corporatists were not interested in protecting working wages. They wanted access to international markets and capital; they wanted the entire economy internationalized. The mega, multi-national corporation was the future, they said, and for that future to arrive, the tariff must go.

The corporatists' ambitions would take time to realize fully. Economic nationalists and elements of the Republican Party continued to advocate the protective tariff as a spur to domestic industry and as a shield for working wages for some years. But in time a new consensus formed, led by academic economists and the professional class. Global integration, they solemnly advised, was not only inevitable but natural, and in fact the only avenue for progress. By the end of the twentieth century, a Republican president would speak rapturously of "open borders, open trade and, most importantly, open minds," as if the three were entirely synonymous.[1] George H. W. Bush, the president in question, went so far as to identify globalization with "the ultimate triumph of mankind," whatever that meant.[2] As the Cold War drew to a close, he called for a new era of global integration, economically and politically. He called it a "new world order."[3] It was the liberal corporatist dream finally come to pass.

In Big Tech, liberal globalism found its ultimate champions. These were companies based in the United States but avowedly multinational in character. They competed in the American market but saw it as secondary to global business. They generated enormously high returns— gaudy and obscene profits for their investors—while employing a tiny number of workers, all things considered.[4] They produced almost nothing, paid next to nothing in U.S. taxes, made virtually no significant capital investments relative to their profits, and extracted nearly all their value as economic rents from a customer base held hostage to their monopoly control.[5] They were the very model of a modern liberal corporation: rent-seeking, extractive, and globalist.

Now there was, one might argue, a certain set of downsides to this business model, a handful of . . . difficulties . . . that gave *some* people pause, those people being generally the working, tax-paying American public. There was Big Tech's enthusiasm, its obsession, its headlong rush to do business in China, on practically any terms dictated by Beijing. There was the industry's determination to locate its supply chains, what few the Big Tech companies had, overseas. There was the fact these corporations seemed somehow to avoid not only national taxes and rules, but any sort of accountability, to anyone. And then there was their anti-competitive conduct, their years-long, billion-dollar efforts to buy out competitors, throttle innovation, take what wasn't theirs, and profit off of other people's work.

In all these ways, Big Tech was the culmination of the corporate liberal ideology and the globalized economy it envisioned. This was an economy that by the early twenty-first century depended less and less on producing anything tangible, or on producers themselves, for that matter, but lavished ever greater rewards on the rarified, highly educated, largely urban technologist class. This was the economy of the "new world order." The economy according to Big Tech.

■ ■ ■

Big Tech's global economic *modus operandi* had three major elements, adding up to a model of extraction practiced on a global scale. To begin, there was Big Tech's aim to achieve maximum market penetration the world over; this was a necessity, according to Big Tech. In a truly worldwide economy, it wasn't enough to excel in a single nation, even one as large as the United States. To achieve maximum profit and optimal economies of scale, a corporate concern needed global access to markets, capital, and labor.

For Big Tech, physical boundaries were unimportant; the Big Tech world was a digital, data-driven place. Tech platforms had no physical product that had to be manufactured or shipped or stored. (Apple had its iPhone and associated items, of course, but it was these *in connection with* its digital App Store platform that gave Apple its reach and relevance.) What made the platforms work was not a physical product, but the closely guarded algorithms. And those needed data. They needed information on a mass scale, millions and billions of data points. The more data, the better the algorithm; the better the algorithm, the more profitable the advertising and sales. And obviously the bigger and more global the audience, the better. To score the backing of big money, the hedge funds and investment bankers, you had to play, or have the potential to play, on a global scale.

Previous global companies had been encumbered with inevitable local commitments—including local factories, local workers, and local regulations and taxes. But Big Tech used its global scale to shed local ties. It was beautifully efficient. Tech's digital nature—the fact it made nothing—meant it could expand into more and more markets without needing to build costly factories or hire costly workers. The only producers the platform companies needed were engineers, and they needed relatively few of them. Jaron Lanier observes, "At the height of its power, the photography company Kodak employed more than 140,000 people and was worth $28 billion. They even invented the first digital camera. But today Kodak is bankrupt, and the new face of digital photography has become Instagram. When Instagram was sold to Facebook for a billion dollars in 2012, it employed only thirteen people."[6] This was progress, globalization style. As for the servers, those supercomputers that made the digital platforms available on any and every screen in the world—these, too, could be operated and maintained by a relative handful of tech workers.[7]

And then there was this: the greater the number of international markets in which the Big Tech platforms played, the more opportunities Big Tech had for arbitrage. That was a fancy, beguiling little word that meant cleverly avoiding taxes and laws. In a strategy that had become utterly *de rigueur* in the globalized economy, the Big Tech companies shifted the location of their profits from one jurisdiction to the next, all electronically, of course, which is to say, fictively, landing on the one that—surprise!—offered the lowest rates. By one estimate, Amazon, Facebook, Google, Netflix, Apple, and Microsoft collectively avoided $100 *billion* in taxes over the last decade. Amazon paid barely any at all.[8]

Which leads to a third feature of Big Tech's globalism: its commitment to steady, predictable returns rather than investment. This preference was, once again, entirely typical of the mega-globalized economy, across industries. Investors preferred their companies as money printers. The less dependent any business was on any one national market, the fewer its local commitments, the more reliably it could generate cold, hard, beautiful cash.

And when it came to generating reliable profits, Big Tech had unique advantages. Big Tech's core business model was built on returns automatically generated by advertising, based on data automatically extracted from users. And it was all done with minimal capital investment by Big Tech.[9] What could be more efficient? Big Tech had become a set of low-labor-cost monopolies subsisting off rents earned with minimal commitment to domestic markets. It was globalized perfection.

It is also, if Big Tech has its way, the future of the global economy. The platforms' aspiration was never growth for the sake of growth. It was never about social media or search or video, either. It was about gaining a foothold in all the highways and byways of social communication the world over that were related in any way to commerce, a foothold that would allow Big Tech to act as gatekeeper, as toll-master, for everything that went across. Put another way, Big Tech seeks to create a global system of automatic rent extraction from the real economy.

This system doesn't stop at the digital world; people still need to *do* things, after all. Man does not live on YouTube clips alone. So Big Tech has established itself as the essential intermediary, the indispensable go-between, to *physical* exchange. Amazon, rare among the tech giants in its willingness to invest its profits, spent years cross-subsidizing its different business lines to ensure it would always be the cheapest choice in retail, until it drove out enough competition to become, effectively, the only choice.[10] The COVID-19 shutdown of physical retailers helped at that. Amazon became a private infrastructure giant, revolutionizing logistics in every industry it touched—grocery, cloud computing, even diapers—and increasingly became the most important outlet for producers.

While Amazon colonized the world of physical commerce, Facebook, in partnership with other tech companies like Uber, had grand plans to replace the venerable United States greenback with its own cryptocurrency, with the ultimate ambition of making Big Tech the intermediary for *all* monetary exchange, wherever it occurred. Facebook's Libra would even facilitate cross-border capital flows, limiting the taxing authority of those dilapidated, worn-out old things called governments, to be replaced by the taxing power of . . . Facebook! When the plan wilted under regulatory scrutiny, Facebook abandoned the project of a new currency in favor of digital equivalents of real dollars, euro, and pounds "to reduce concerns around monetary sovereignty." It "retired" its first Libra white paper, replacing all references in the Libra mission statement to a new "simple global currency" with the phrase "simple global payment system," hoping regulators might forget its ambitions.[11]

What it all amounted to, over time, was the steady transfer of wealth from actual producers, actual working people, to technologists and other members of their class. For years, working-class wages in the United States had flatlined or fallen, while gains in income and wealth pooled into the elite circles of Big Tech and Big Finance.[12] The expansion of the Big Tech economy threatens to accelerate these trends and make them permanent, which means a future where Big Tech's vast returns flow into a few silos in Silicon Valley and Seattle and Wall Street while working Americans' jobs are exported to cheaper labor markets. And *that* means that not only do the Big Tech barons and their investors benefit from this model of economic globalization, but so do countries with cheaper labor markets that absorb manufacturing jobs and production plants—China, in particular.

■ ■ ■

Since China won permanent normal trade relations with the United States in 2000 and membership in the World Trade Organization a year later, Americans have lost over 3 million jobs to the People's Republic, as company after company followed the Big Tech playbook.[13]

In the 2000s and 2010s, Facebook, Google, and Apple all desperately sought access to China's domestic market. Apple had the most success. It won the right to sell its products there, and China quickly became one of Apple's biggest and most important markets. Apple agreed to store the encryption keys to China-based Apple devices *in China*, putting them under the watchful eye of the Chinese Communist Party.[14] And the keys weren't just on Chinese soil; they were placed under the control of a Chinese state-owned enterprise, China Telecom.[15] In addition, Apple located most of its production supply chains in China, for a simple reason: wages were cheaper in China. This was especially true when one used forced labor, as one recent report strongly suggests Apple did, by relying in part on labor sourced from concentration camps in the Xinjiang province.[16] On Capitol Hill, Apple is among the most vigorous corporate actors lobbying behind the scenes against legislative efforts to crack down on Uighur slave labor.[17]

As for Google and Facebook, both made frantic plays for Chinese market access. Google went so far as to develop an alternate search engine for China, dubbed Google.cn, which would exclude from search returns such political topics as the Tiananmen Square massacre, the mass murders of the so-called Cultural Revolution, or the treatment of the Muslim Uighurs in Xinjiang. China ultimately refused to play ball, however, preferring instead to invest in domestic counterparts, in keeping with its formula of authoritarian capitalism. But not before Google prostrated itself in a years-long dalliance.[18]

Facebook, too, toyed with censorship to please the Chinese Communists, including developing internal software to enforce China's blatant anti-speech laws.[19] Mark Zuckerberg got in on the act personally, launching a direct and high-profile courtship of Chinese officials, even while the Chinese government routed billions of renminbi through state-owned banks and government funds to a Facebook competitor.[20]

This was the globalized, corporate liberal economy at full throttle: selling out American production, compromising Americans' data, censoring on behalf of Communists, employing forced labor (or looking the other way while your business partners did so), and courting dictators, all for market domination.

And then there was what Big Tech was willing to do to maintain the market power it already had.

■ ■ ■

Big Tech's army of paid sycophants in Washington loved to expound on the sanctity of the free market; Big Tech being supposedly a product of that market. In fact, no corporate actors had done more to undermine competition and free enterprise than Big Tech. That's the thing about plutocrats: once they seize the power, they tend to keep it. While Big Tech's rhetoric all came from the corporate liberal songbook of freedom and choice, its actions worked to entrench its own domination.

Google was the most brazen of the bunch. Beginning in the 2010s, Google systematically ripped off the platform functionality and even content of smaller online rivals and incorporated them into its own products, a series of specialty platforms like Google Shopping and Google Travel.[21] Not content merely to dominate the world of internet search—90 percent of all web searches in the world are performed with Google—the company moved to eliminate all competition and, in particular, to kill a set of small specialty platforms with search engines that focused on delivering one type of product: Kayak and Orbitz for travel, for example, Yelp for local reviews. Google wanted them gone.

It wasn't that these small specialty platforms posed much of a threat to Google Search. Google was a search monstrosity; they were pygmies. But Google wanted *all* search on the internet, for *any* product or service, to run through its Search platform. Google wanted total control, so it targeted these small, recalcitrant little platforms for elimination, and then cut a few corners. It cloned the most successful of them, scraped their content right from their pages, and then repackaged it all as . . . Google.[22] Next Google gave preference to these new "Google" services in its search results. The power of Google's search dominance coupled with its self-dealing practices ran the smaller platforms right into irrelevance.[23]

In 2017, the European Union fined Google 2.42 billion euro for its anti-competitive conduct, finding that "Google has systematically given prominent placement to its own comparison shopping service" while it "demoted rival comparison shopping services in its search results."[24] A follow-on report in the *Wall Street Journal* in 2020 disclosed that Google similarly gave preference to videos from YouTube (which it owns) over competitors' videos in search results, even when the latter were more popular.[25]

In 2018, the European Commission fined Google another whopping 4.34 billion euro for anti-competition violations related to its Android phone and operating systems. The commission found that Google paid Android manufacturers to pre-load Google Search and its web browser, Chrome, on Android phones to keep off any rivals. Google forced the same manufacturers to pre-load Google's app store, called Google Play, threatening that if they didn't, Google would block phone purchasers from downloading the app store later, grossly diminishing the value of the phone. The threat worked, and Google profited.[26]

And then there was Google's abuse of the advertising market, its prized cash cow. That market is composed of several layers of software and other technology connecting advertisers with wares to sell to publishers with advertising space to offer. Insiders call the system "the ad stack," and a comprehensive report from the United Kingdom's competition agency in 2020 concluded that Google exercised a dominant position in every segment of it.[27] Meaning that Google represented *both* the buyers *and* the sellers in the ad market, ran both the buyer and seller ad platforms, and even ran the digital exchange where the price of ad space was determined. And it used this dominance to its own advantage, naturally. On the supply side, Google "increase[d] its market power at the publisher ad server level by making it difficult to access Google [advertiser] demand through non-Google ad servers." On the demand side, it "used its position as the largest publisher ad server to favour its own demand . . . for example, by penalising third-party [buyers]."[28] In similar fashion, Google leveraged the popularity of its dominant video platform, YouTube, and the popularity of Google Search to induce advertisers who wanted to place ads in those places—and who didn't?—to use Google to purchase display ads in other spaces, from other publishers. In this fashion, Google converted its dominance in video and search into dominance in advertising, forcing competitors out of business.[29]

The European Union eventually fined Google for its advertising misbehavior to the tune of 1.5 billion euro, concluding the company's conduct was, once again, anti-competitive and contrary to law.[30] Based on this evidence and other, similar allegations, the U.S. Department of Justice launched an antitrust investigation of Google in 2019, along with—finally—all fifty state attorneys general. The Justice Department filed a formal antitrust enforcement suit in November of 2020.[31]

Google may have been the most flagrant miscreant, but Facebook was no slouch. The titan of social media achieved market dominance by promising users something it later systematically denied them, privacy, and it maintained that dominance by purchasing would-be competitors. Facebook entered the social media market in 2004 by pledging to give users the sort of social-networking opportunities other sites already offered, but with something extra: personal privacy protections. It was a deliberate marketing strategy. At the time, MySpace dominated the social media world, but users worried that its lax privacy protections permitted exploitation of children and teens.[32] Facebook would do everything MySpace could do, but with strict privacy settings that shielded its users. Facebook even promised not to track its customers around the web.

The promises had an effect. By the end of the decade, Facebook had overtaken MySpace as the web's dominant social platform, and in due course would drive MySpace, and every other major competitor, into extinction. But early on, Facebook became adept at doing just the opposite of what it promised its users. It became an expert in surveillance. Indeed, in 2012 Facebook agreed to settle a Federal Trade Commission inquiry into multiple privacy violations, including allegations that the company had changed privacy settings for users without their consent, allowed applications more access to user information than Facebook had disclosed, misled users about the degree to which the customer privacy controls actually limited Facebook's access to data, lied about its efforts to verify the security of the apps it offered, and shared personal data with advertisers after telling users it wouldn't.[33] Then in 2019, Facebook agreed to pay $5 *billion* in fines for violating the earlier consent decree.[34] Privacy had been a key component of Facebook's competitive strategy, but it had been a lie.

Meanwhile, after banishing MySpace, Facebook set about purchasing potential competitors, most famously Instagram and WhatsApp. Mark Zuckerberg was uncharacteristically frank about his intentions, saying in one email exchange with a top Facebook executive that the whole point of these acquisitions was to scotch the competition. "These businesses are nascent but the networks established, the brands are already meaningful, and if they grow to a large scale they could be very disruptive to us," he wrote. "I'm curious if we should consider going after one or two of them." Zuckerberg's plan was to "buy these companies and leave their products running while over time incorporating the social dynamics they've invented into our core products."[35] In short, buy the competitors and roll them into Facebook. And that's what Facebook did.

By 2019, Facebook was under investigation—again—by the Federal Trade Commission, this time for its acquisition of Instagram and WhatsApp, while forty-seven attorneys general probed the company's manipulation of advertising prices.[36]

Apple and Amazon were equally aggressive, some might say *predatory*, in defense of their respective market shares. Apple's major platform was the App Store, where it sold the clever software gadgets and gizmos for its famous phone (and iPad, and computers). The App Store was a closed universe, and designed to be—only Apple-approved applications could be sold there, and Apple's App Store was the only store available to Apple device users. (This was in contrast to Android users, who could purchase apps from multiple competing application stores.) Apple capitalized on this closed-system arrangement to charge application designers who wanted to sell their products in Apple's store a little something, or perhaps a large something, or perhaps 30 percent of all sales and subscriptions. The price tag dropped to 15 percent after the first subscription year, and Apple offered special terms to certain developers (like Amazon), but app designers complained nonetheless, labeling it the "Apple Tax."[37]

One major app designer, Spotify, alleged in litigation that this tax, along with Apple's self-preferment in the Apple Store, has prevented it from competing with Apple on fair terms.[38] Spotify has a music streaming service. So does Apple, which it introduced based in part on, yes, Spotify's model. To give its own product a little boost, Apple limited Spotify's ability to integrate its music streaming with the rest of Apple's iPhone operating system and the broader Apple product line.[39] Spotify wasn't the only one to notice Apple's self-dealing. A *Wall Street Journal* analysis in 2019 discovered that Apple ranked its own applications first in the App Store, ahead of competitors, a powerful advantage that skirted, if not downright trampled, the company's own rules and statements on rankings.[40]

By 2020, Apple's efforts to curb competition had drawn the scrutiny of European antitrust officials, who launched reviews of the App Store, including the so-called Apple Tax, as well as of Apple's management of its "Apple Pay" payment system.[41]

Amazon, not satisfied with killing off local stores and traditional retailers, had begun ripping off the vendors on its own platform by the late 2010s, or so complaints to the Federal Trade Commission alleged.[42] Amazon used data gleaned from third-party sellers on its site to launch its own competing brand of staple items, called Amazon Basics—and then gave preference to Amazon Basics in the search results. The FTC complaint alleged Amazon went further yet, tying the prominence of a third-party seller's products in the Amazon search results to that seller's purchase of other Amazon services, like its cloud-computing operation, Amazon Web Services (AWS).[43]

Those tactics weren't new. Amazon was already notorious for forcing its sellers to agree never to offer lower prices at other outlets or on other platforms. Amazon was known to employ ruthless tactics to stamp out online start-ups, especially those offering staple items.[44] It built its proprietary digital services using parts of open-source code from third-party developers.[45] And Amazon famously played hardball in contract negotiations with vendors by slowing delivery of orders to extract pricing and other concessions.[46] The company even allowed counterfeit products to thrive in its store to force sellers like Nike, which preferred to manage distribution itself, to play ball. Even after Nike gave in and offered its shoes on Amazon's storefront, the counterfeit sales continued.[47] It was simple power politics. Given the size of its audience—almost 40 percent of online commerce in America moved across its platform—and the reach of its distribution channels, Amazon could single-handedly cripple the companies with which it did business.[48] And it wasn't afraid to try.

■ ■ ■

The Big Tech barons extolled themselves as the harbingers of a new world, a fairer, more peaceful, better-informed order that was truly *global*. In an open letter to the "Facebook community" in February 2017, Mark Zuckerberg used the word "global" twelve times in the introduction alone. "Our greatest opportunities are now global," he enthused, "like spreading prosperity and freedom." And: "Our greatest challenges also need global responses." And in case anyone missed the point: "Progress now requires humanity coming together not just as cities or nations, but also as a global community."[49] It was the globalizing ambitions of the corporate liberals finally brought to their apex. Tech's model of extraction-based globalism reflected the priorities of the corporate liberal order, as well as the consensus of Western policy-makers in thrall to the corporate vision. Tech was (supposedly) a textbook example of how to succeed in the age of globalization.

But Big Tech was also a case study in the transfer of power that mega-globalization achieved. Leaders as diverse as President George H. W. Bush and Facebook's Mark Zuckerberg spoke of prosperity and democracy almost interchangeably, of a globalism of "open borders, open trade . . . and open minds," as if the expanding global market were synonymous with freedom and self-government. Woodrow Wilson had similarly and frequently linked international cooperation and multilateral policy with the spread of democracy, as if those things were somehow the same. But they are not.

In practice, the Big Tech–led age of economic globalism has weakened democracy rather than strengthened it. It has done so by eroding the standing of those Americans once thought central to the republic—working- and middle-class Americans. It exported many of their jobs, limited their future prospects, and left their towns and neighborhoods to wither. And all the while, it entrenched the power of Big Tech.

By 2020, a few tech denizens were beginning to feel a certain unease, even a sense of responsibility regarding this state of affairs. But their solution, memorialized in the presidential campaign of tech guru Andrew Yang, was not to question corporate liberal globalism or the basic business model of Big Tech, not to recover the independence of working Americans, but to pay those unfortunate workers to be obsolete. Pay them to make their livelihoods, their families, and their futures utterly dependent on the coalition of Big Tech and Big Government. Yang and his supporters in Silicon Valley called it "universal basic income," a guaranteed monthly payment to those whom the globalized economy had left out. But a more accurate term would have been "universal dependence on the good graces of Big Tech." It was the ultimate corporate liberal proposal and the ultimate inversion of the republican ideal. The laboring class would no longer control the economy, no longer define the interests of the nation, no longer practice self-government in any meaningful sense. No, the corporate elite would manage it all now, control it all—and look after America's (former) workers as their wards.

CHAPTER 9

RIGGING WASHINGTON

The founding generation believed aristocracy was never happenstance, never natural or inevitable. It was a political choice, the outcome of policy. J. P. Morgan and the corporate barons of his time had argued the reverse: that an aristocracy of monopolists was inevitable in the modern age. But their decades-long quest for political power—lobbying, pressuring, bribing politicians when all else failed—suggested otherwise. They needed the power of government to carry out their program. They needed government to consolidate their power. A century later, the Big Tech barons have learned the lesson well. They too want to use the power of government to cement their status as the new corporate elite. And I can testify to that firsthand.

In the spring of 2019, soon after arriving in the Senate, I proposed to limit one of the major subsidies the tech industry gets from government, a shield from legal liability offered especially to Big Tech. I was merely a first-year senator, no seniority, no fancy committee chairmanships, and yet, the response was ferocious.

Big Tech promptly mobilized its legions of lobbyists and think-tank apologists and chattering acolytes in the press to search, fix, and destroy my legislation, to incinerate it, and to send a message, as mafiosos do, that anyone who would dare challenge Big Tech's supremacy would be incinerated alongside. And so it began, broadsides in the press, takedowns in the blogosphere, and wave upon wave of visits from "concerned" lobbyists—"concerned" as in, "We're very concerned for *your future.*"

Big Tech's frantic reaction to even one senator's challenge to its power suggested to me several things. First, Big Tech had bought enormous influence in the hallowed precincts of Washington, D.C. Second, Big Tech was (and is) desperate to protect its special relationship, its sweetheart deals, with Big Government. Big Tech has not grown big on its own, and the tech barons know it. Third, and perhaps most revealing, Big Tech is desperately afraid of public criticism, of someone taking a public stand. It worries night and day that one break in the dyke will cause the whole edifice to collapse, and therefore spends inordinate sums of time and money to preserve a consensus of elite opinion that tech power is untouchable, inevitable, progressive. You know the line.

Big Tech's reaction convinced me not only that I was on the right course in criticizing the special treatment it received, but that the *alliance* of Big Tech and Big Government must be broken. To challenge the Big Tech corporate aristocracy, we must challenge the political choices that brought it to power.

■ ■ ■

The Communications Decency Act, adopted in 1996, has inadvertently become a massive federal subsidy, worth hundreds of billions of dollars, for Big Tech. The internet was in its infancy then, long before today's major platforms arrived on the scene, long before the advent of social media. AOL was the largest internet service provider, and to get an internet connection, the average American had to connect a phone line to the back of her computer (a giant hulk of a thing, with a separate monitor and disk drive and keyboard), drag the line over to the wall, unplug her telephone from the jack and snap the computer-connected phone line into its place, and then . . . dial up. It was, digitally speaking, a land before time.

Congress's principal concern in those days was to keep the internet from being overrun with pornography—and child predators, child exploitation, and smut in general. Enter the Communications Decency Act. The point of the law, as its lead sponsor in the Senate said at the time, was "to provide much-needed protection for children."[1] It imposed liability on internet companies that displayed "obscene" or "indecent" material to minors. Unfortunately, at least one court of law had previously held that any internet company that moderated the content of its users—even in the service of pruning legally dubious content—would then become liable to suit for any and all content on its site from third parties, whether illicit or not.[2] In the jargon of the law, blocking out smut might render an internet provider a "publisher" of all the material of all its users, making the provider subject to suit for users' content.

That's when Congress hit upon a fix. It would provide internet companies with immunity from such lawsuits. So in a section of the Communications Decency Act that was to have an illustrious later life, Section 230, Congress provided that an internet company that merely *edits* some content does not thereby become a "publisher." It is liable only for the content it edits or develops. Congress further provided that when an internet provider *removes* content—as with the new statutory mandate against obscenity—the provider is not liable to suit if it acts in "good faith." This appeared to be an elegant solution, encouraging internet providers to remove indecent material without exposing them to legal liability.

Big Tech loved this solution—but wanted more, more immunity, no strings attached, and went to court to get it. The U.S. Supreme Court got the redrafting effort underway barely a year after the Communications Decency Act became law. It struck down as unconstitutional the requirement that tech companies remove obscenity—but left intact Big Tech's legal immunity from suit, something no other media companies enjoyed.[3] And still Big Tech wanted more.

Big Tech wanted to further expand its legal immunity by eliminating the distinction between publishers and distributors of content. When it passed the Communications Decency Act, Congress recognized that an internet provider that helped "develop" or edit content should face the same level of liability that a newspaper would for material it edited and published; in this regard, internet companies were in fact "publishers."[4] But if the internet company merely posted or passed along third-party content without change, acting as a "distributor," the company was liable only if it knew, or should have known, the material was illegal.

At Big Tech's behest, the courts soon changed this entire framework. They dramatically narrowed what behavior counted as publishing, granting internet companies broad discretion to make editorial decisions, including altering content, *without* becoming liable for the content they altered.[5] Then courts nullified the "good faith" requirement in the law for *taking down* content. Section 230 had required that internet companies act in "good faith," evenhandedly, with justifiable and non-discriminatory reasons, when they removed content from their platforms.[6] But now the courts said they could take down content without needing to show good faith in the least.[7] Finally, courts eliminated the requirement that distributors refrain from displaying material they know or should know is illegal.[8]

Such that when all was said and done, when the dust had cleared from this strenuous bout of judicial renovation, Section 230 had been completely rewritten. Under the new and improved statute, tech companies could shape or edit content without liability, could take down content without any show of good faith or fair dealing, and could display content they knew to be illegal—and no one could challenge any of it in court. No other media concerns—no newspaper, no television network, no entertainment or film company—enjoyed this kind of immunity.

The value of this redrafted statute was very nearly incalculable. Behind the shield of Section 230, Google and Facebook and Amazon proceeded to build the modern digital platform, that amalgam of shared user content, for-profit advertising, product sales, and journalism all in one place. This was a feat that required significant shaping, editing, alteration, and removal of third-party content, which the tech platforms did, all without liability.

Thanks to Section 230, tech could produce nothing and control everything. Users would do the real work of production, and tech's algorithms would tweak and amplify that content for optimal engagement—no human supervision required by law; no genuine, journalistic editorial oversight; no redress available for anyone harmed by it all. Big Tech would have all the power to control information flow with none of the responsibility that the common law would demand of any corporate actor in a similar role of influence in the physical world. It was as if the government had given tomorrow's drug lords a new pharmacological formula *and* a promise that they couldn't be sued for what happened in the opium dens they ran. And that was the point. No company could possibly wield this sort of power—no one would dare to try—if the law imposed liability on it for its misuse.

When the tech behemoths claim, as they routinely do, that they couldn't exist without Section 230, they are only slightly exaggerating. They couldn't exist without the new and improved Section 230 that they rewrote with the help of the courts. Without this redrafted 230 we might have had something different—a system of decentralized, open-source, pro-privacy communications protocols for peer-to-peer messaging and user-curated content feeds. We might have had a larger and healthier content production ecosystem, buoyed by the traffic of the internet but without the platform rents and control. We might have had a set of online tools for video hosting, blogging, and shopping to make user-generated content available to users without thrusting it on them by means of a corporate recommendation engine.

We might have had all that. Instead, Section 230 gave Big Tech the means to constrict the global flow of information. Big Tech's handouts from Big Government made the tech class what it is.

■ ■ ■

Should someone, anyone, have the temerity to *challenge* this arrangement, to point out the sweetheart deal Big Tech has managed to obtain for itself from the nation's government, well, prepare to face the wrath of Big Tech's other form of alliance with the political class, its phalanx of lobbyists, think-tankers, and paid mouthpieces in the media and academe.

Google and its fellow tech platforms have spent millions purchasing insider influence, as I learned firsthand when I proposed to end Big Tech's special treatment under the revised Section 230. It started happening almost immediately, a chorus of criticism in the nation's newspapers of record and from think-tank "experts" and professors (some of them formerly employed by the federal government to *regulate* the tech platforms).

These various groups and personages had two things in common, I soon discovered. They were all card-carrying members of the Washington elite, or more precisely, that particular segment of the elite that does not itself occupy office or make any actual decisions but buzzes about those who do, communicating the official position of the wise, the learned, the experts. These people were, in short, *courtiers*. That was the first thing. The second was that they were all paid by Big Tech.

In Washington, it's always wise to follow the money, and Big Tech has spent handsomely to buy the good graces and the chattering mouths of the Washington courtier set. Google, for instance, has shoveled millions of dollars to hundreds of nonprofit groups across the political spectrum in order to purchase influence—at least 350 different groups as of 2019, a who's who of the professional talkers in Washington, including the American Antitrust Institute, the American Enterprise Institute, the Brookings Institution, the Cato Institute, the Heritage Foundation, Americans for Tax Reform, and the U.S. Chamber of Commerce.[9] And Google's giving has paid dividends. One *New York Times* report recorded privacy advocates' concerns: "Google's willingness to spread cash around the think tanks and advocacy groups focused on internet and telecommunications policy has effectively muted, if not silenced, criticism of the company. . . ."[10] According to privacy advocates, "[I]t has become increasingly difficult to find partners" to call out privacy violations "as more groups accept Google funding."[11]

In other words, Google and the rest weren't spreading around all this cash out of the goodness of their hearts. Case in point, the New America Foundation, a sleek outfit based in Washington that employs a gaggle of fellows with sparkling resumes and a long list of television appearances and boasts that its mission is to renew "the promise of America by continuing the quest to realize our nation's highest ideals."[12] A mission it pursues by accepting tech company cash, including more than $21 million from Google alone.[13]

And what happens when a New America fellow, one of those "innovative problem-solvers" who "prize [their] intellectual and ideological independence," in the words of the New America Foundation itself, ventures the tiniest criticism of the Big Tech empire?[14] In 2017, the president of New America ousted a senior foundation scholar, *his entire staff, and the center he ran* after the scholar posted a statement in support of the European Union's antitrust penalty against Google. It seems Google executive chairman Eric Schmidt—who has his own conference room at New America, the "Eric Schmidt Ideas Lab"—had seen the criticism and was, to put it mildly, not amused. These were not the kind of ideas he was paying for. Shortly thereafter, the offending scholar, his staff, and the center they ran—the "Open Markets Initiative"—were gone.[15]

Besides their massive investments in the nonprofit world, the tech giants sink tens of millions into professional lobbyists, with Google's parent company, Alphabet, spending nearly $22 million on lobbying in just one calendar year, 2018, and $90 million since 2015. Not to be left behind, Facebook has shelled out about $75 million in the same time frame, Amazon nearly $79 million, and Apple $36 million. Flacking for Big Tech is, it seems, an industry unto itself.[16]

And then there are the academics, the professional economists and antitrust experts the tech giants pay to sing their praises. Over the past decade, Google has financed hundreds of research papers defending the company against charges of antitrust violations and from other regulatory initiatives, sometimes shelling out as much as $400,000 per project.[17] The researchers who get this cash frequently permit Google to review the papers before they are published or peer-reviewed, a major no-no in the academic world—but with this much cash involved, who's to judge? Google then promotes said "research" to government officials, going so far as to pay the travel expenses for the academics to meet with congressional staffers and executive branch officials.[18]

The tech giants have even tried their hand at funding whole faculties. Amazon, Google, and other tech-sector stalwarts, like Qualcomm, have together ponied up millions to fund George Mason University's Global Antitrust Institute, a grandly titled if perhaps misnamed endeavor. The Global Antitrust Institute churns out papers supportive of Big Tech and is presided over, no surprise, by a former antitrust lawyer for Google. But what truly sets the institute apart is its aggressive courtship of government regulators, the people supposedly enforcing the nation's privacy and antitrust laws. At one recent conference in swanky Huntington Beach, California, the institute wined and dined more than thirty government officials, foreign and domestic, who have charge over competition laws. The attendees spent entire days in "classes" with the institute's faculty, where the chief lesson was: don't regulate Big Tech. These sessions included a former member of the Federal Trade Commission and a senior federal judge. And in case anyone missed the point, the assigned reading included a paper by our old friend Hal Varian, Google's chief economist, the gist of which was that antitrust law does not apply to tech companies.[19]

Big Tech has bought itself quite a chorus in the nation's capital, one ready to sing lustily at Big Tech's command. And it apparently includes the regulators themselves.

■ ■ ■

Responsibility for enforcing the country's antitrust and competition laws is somewhat awkwardly divided between the Department of Justice and the Federal Trade Commission, which Woodrow Wilson created in 1914 to regulate the great corporations. The FTC is, by design, accountable to no one in particular—exactly the sort of institute of experts corporate liberals favor. Due to the unclear division of authority between the FTC and the Justice Department, it is the FTC that has taken the lead on antitrust and competition issues in recent years, and it has used that enforcement authority to accomplish . . . well, nothing in particular. Because while the FTC is nominally an "independent" agency, it is not, it turns out, independent of Big Tech.

A recent study by a watchdog group found that two-thirds of top FTC officials either were affiliated with Big Tech before they arrived or became lawyers or lobbyists for top tech companies after they left the agency, including six FTC chairs and nine directors of the FTC Bureau of Competition. Washington is full of "revolving door" employees who move from federal positions to private practice and back again, and the FTC is no exception.[20]

Maybe that's why, in 2012, FTC commissioners ignored Bureau of Competition investigative staff who reported that Google had "used anticompetitive tactics and abused its monopoly power." The staff formally urged the FTC's governing board, the commissioners, to bring an enforcement lawsuit challenging Google's practices. The investigative team concluded Google's "conduct has resulted—and will result—in real harm to consumers and to innovation in the online search and advertising markets."[21] The staff report found Google had illegally stolen content from rival platforms like Yelp, Tripadivsor, and even Amazon to improve its own services.[22]

It was bombshell stuff, the kind of evidence that could have blown open Big Tech, that could have launched the biggest antitrust case since the case against Microsoft two decades earlier, maybe the biggest since the breakup of AT&T. But it never happened. A week after FTC investigators began issuing subpoenas for documents related to the case, Google hired *twelve* new lobbying firms. And then Google really got down to business. The company tapped every connection, called in every favor, and activated every ounce of influence it possessed in every corner it could reach. And its reach was impressive. In the days following the

FTC investigative report, Google representatives sat down repeatedly with FTC officials to try and clear up this unfortunate misunderstanding. And they did . . . at the White House.[23]

Google was the second-largest source of corporate contributions to President Barack Obama's 2012 campaign.[24] White House logs revealed that Google executives were frequent visitors to the president's mansion. Google was on the inside of the inside; it had a line all the way to the top, to the very apex of American government. And now it used it. Google cofounder Larry Page met personally with FTC officials on November 27, 2012, to urge a settlement. Three days later, Google chairman Eric Schmidt went directly to the White House for a sit-down with President Obama's senior advisor on tech issues. At about the same time, a senior FTC aide told other staff members, "We're going to start our settlement discussions with Google."[25] Within a few weeks, it was a done deal. In January 2013, the FTC commissioners voted unanimously to shut down the Google investigation. No suit. No charges.[26]

The corporate-liberal government by experts turned out to be government by the well-connected on behalf of the well-funded. In a word, government of, by, and for the elite. This was the power of access. Tech bought it, built it, marshaled it, and deployed it at every level of government, in every corridor of power in Washington, D.C. Like the robber barons before them, the tech class was willing to take no chances with its suzerainty. Eternal vigilance and truckloads of cash were the price of dominance.

The American founders advocated a political economy of republicanism to protect the rule of the common man. But this was a political economy of aristocracy. The tech barons wanted to control the economy, the media, news, politics . . . all of it, remaking the nation in their image. As for the republic, that grand experiment in self-government by the common man and woman—that would fade away, recede into the mists of history, unobtrusively, quietly, such that no one would really notice, to be replaced once and for all by the rule of the corporate elite.

PART III

CHAPTER 10

WHAT EACH OF US CAN DO

Big Tech looms as large as any corporate power in American history, as large as the railroads from a century back, as large as the steel trust and the oil trust and the money trust from the height of the Gilded Age. Its sway is prodigious; its reach is wide. And yet, like those earlier monopolies, Big Tech's power is ultimately precarious, because Americans are never long contented to be ruled over by barons. They agitate, they protest. They rebel against it. That is what is happening now. And that is why there is cause for hope.

It is possible to imagine a world where tech serves us, and not the other way around, where the Big Tech monopolies are monopolies no longer, where our property in our personal data is protected, where our children are safe online, where our speech is free. This is possible because Americans have not yet given up the ambition to govern themselves, to be the masters of their own fates. There lives in the common man and woman, the citizens of the great American middle, great strength yet.

It is possible to imagine a future beyond corporate liberalism. That political economy has dominated American life for a century now, through war and peace and the advent of the digital age, but it has not served America well. It has steadily eroded the power and standing of the working class. It has steadily widened our class divisions and installed a professional elite at the prow of society, an elite that grows further removed from the lives and aspirations of working people with every passing year. In exchange, corporate liberalism has offered the personal freedom of personal choice, the liberty of self-expression and consumption. It has pushed aside the liberty connected to self-government, and deliberately so. And in so doing, the political economy of corporate liberalism has threatened the republic itself; it has threatened the self-rule of the common man and woman. Corporate liberalism turns out to be a political economy of aristocracy, very much of the kind the founders feared and warned against, of the kind the Populists remonstrated against and Theodore Roosevelt resisted, and it has been with us now for a century too long. The battle to end the tyranny of Big Tech is ultimately a battle to break the hold of corporate liberalism.

It can be done. We can do it, we the people. We can do it by taking personal action, in our homes and with our families, by making the real social world, the life of family and neighborhood and civic association, a powerful counterweight to Big Tech's ambition to hook us on its platforms and control our lives. And we can do it by making different political choices—by revitalizing antitrust legislation, ending the corporate giveaways, protecting our fundamental constitutional right to free speech, and revising our overall economic and social policy to put working people first.

■ ■ ■

We can start in our own lives. Ending Big Tech's sovereignty is about taking back our own, and we can begin to do that in the lives we live together. Big Tech works relentlessly to force individuals into its ecosystem of addiction, exhibitionism, and fear of missing out. It seeks to create its own social universe and draw all of life into its orbit. But the real social world, the life of family and neighborhood—the authentic communities that sustain authentic togetherness—can act as a counter-weight to Big Tech's ambitions. They can act as what they always have been, as havens for individuals and as training grounds for citizens. If these real and authentic communities have grown weak in recent decades in the political economy of corporate liberalism, that is no reason to abandon their potential now. In fact, it is just the time to reclaim them. And the place to start is the family.

One of my favorite political thinkers is the Dutch theologian and one-time prime minister of the Netherlands (1901–1905), Abraham Kuyper. One of Kuyper's central convictions was that the truest foundation for freedom, personal and political, is the sovereignty of the family. "The starting point" in ordering the "affairs of state and society," he said, "should be in the family."[1] The idea of sovereignty conveys power, and that was just what Kuyper meant. Our families have a power and a weight all their own, strong enough to help make us who we are and strong enough to resist malign influences.

I am myself a husband and a father, with three small children at home, all under the age of eight. Like all parents, my wife, Erin, and I had to make decisions early on about screen time in our home—and then revise those decisions in the light of experience. With our first son, we initially permitted him a fair amount of screen time to play games and watch programs. We *hoped* they would be educational programs. We steered him to ones that were allegedly helpful in child development, as recommended by friends and fellow parents. We even considered getting him an iPad. Most families we knew did that for their children, and many elementary schools make extensive use of mobile platforms. It all seemed normal.

But we soon noticed that the more screen time our small son had, the more screen time he wanted; he was especially drawn to the interactive nature of the iPad and iPhone, with their bells and whistles and colors and notifications. Television was boring by comparison. The Apple products were like, well, slot machines—flashing lights, chiming bells, buttons to press! When my wife at one point got a new iPhone, we briefly thought about giving our son the old one, stripped of its cell plan, to be used as a tool for interactive learning games. He was so mesmerized by the possibility that he started excitedly telling every person with whom he came into contact that he was going to get an iPhone of his own. That's when we began to read more deeply into the effects of these devices on kids. And what we found led us to an about-face. Rather than getting him an iPad or a phone, we decided to stop exposing him to mobile devices altogether. By the time our younger son came along, we had established a routine: the kids could watch a (very) limited amount of television each week, but mobile devices were forbidden.

Instead, we learned to prioritize other things, other means of education, engagement, and entertainment. Our boys are very active (and we suspect our daughter, who has only just arrived, will be too!). Rather than looking at screens, we found active things we could do together— playing in the backyard, going to parks, building forts. We made time to read together as a family, usually right before bed now that the boys have started school. Keeping them off screens is still a challenge, especially when they are with friends. But we have found that just as screen time feeds an appetite for more, the reverse is also true. The *less* contact our children have with interactive devices, the *less* interested they are in them; they find other activities that involve real human interaction more rewarding. And we decided to allow our kids absolutely zero personal contact with social media. They don't know what Facebook means—and we hope to keep it that way as long as possible. Real friends are the priority, not Facebook friends.

Erin and I found that the biggest challenge to shielding our family from the influence of Big Tech was . . . us. I use a smartphone, as does she, and both of us use smart tablets and personal computers and have social media accounts. It was one thing to keep my boys off mobile devices and social media, but the healthy rhythm of our family life was no less threatened by my constantly looking at screens. I could rationalize it, of course. I needed it for work. I had to stay connected. I needed to keep my phone with me always—just in case. Around the time Erin and

I decided to make our home device-free for our kids, I started tracking more closely my own habits. I noticed I was taking the phone with me to the dinner table. To the park. It was in my pocket when I was wrestling with the boys or reading to them. If our family was truly going to be a haven from Big Tech's influence, then I realized I had to change my own behavior. As much as my kids, I needed to get away from Big Tech and its domination of our lives.

Now when I come home from work, I plug my phone in to recharge it on a counter away from the family—and leave it until we've put the kids to bed. When we go out to eat together, I leave the phone in the car. I enlisted the kids' help to police me: if they saw me with a phone at the dinner table, they were to shout, "Dad, put that phone down!" They loved it, and it was effective.

As for social media, I do use it, but again within limits. I don't post when I'm at home and the kids are awake. When I do post something to Twitter or Facebook, I force myself to post and log off; I don't want to be drawn into the mire of the social media ecosystem. In the mornings, I don't check my phone until I've taken some quiet time to reflect, pray, and set the day's agenda; increasingly, I try to limit my screen time during the day by checking my texts and emails only at designated intervals. I have switched off all notification sounds, badges, and alerts on my personal devices to keep interruptions to a minimum, and I have friends who have gone further, turning off the color on their cell phones because a black-and-white screen diminishes its allure. Some have disabled the Autoplay feature on YouTube so that one video does not lead ceaselessly to the next. Others never leave their phones at their bedside tables. These are all good ideas.

Adults and families need to make their own choices about what works for them and what doesn't. Some research suggests, for example, that limited amounts of screen time on mobile devices can be good for early childhood development. Some people can't limit their media usage in the ways I try to; others find different patterns more helpful. You will know what is best for your family and your situation. I share my experience only to illustrate the kinds of choices every family has to grapple with, and the pressures they encounter. Above all, every family faces the pressure stoked by Big Tech to acquiesce and allow the tech platforms to intrude into every corner of family life. But there is real value to be gained in saying no to Big Tech's incursions, and tremendous potential when we do it together as families. I know some families with older children who have ditched social media altogether. Others skip it periodically; they call it a family social media "fast." Another friend keeps a basket for cell phones near the front door of her house, encouraging visiting friends and family to temporarily surrender their phones and be free from tech distractions. Erin and I have started doing this too.

Just as important as eliminating Big Tech distractions is cultivating a counter-rhythm of family togetherness. In our home, family dinners are a touchstone of our life together. I make every effort to be home at dinnertime with my family so we can sit down together—with no phones! There is no substitute for this unhurried, face-to-face time of sharing, laughing, and relating. And with two small boys and a new baby, I can assure you that dinnertimes in our house are wild and adventurous affairs! Other families prioritize breakfast in this way, before kids and parents disperse. But whether it's breakfast or dinner or some other touchpoint during the day, rituals of family togetherness are an effective counterweight to the isolating, atomizing influence of Big Tech.

Families are one center of influence to counter Big Tech's power. Another is the authentic community of neighborhoods and schools and houses of worship. Block parties, holiday gatherings, even just neighborhood kids playing together—all these little things are important. They build a sense of connection and place—rootedness—that weakens the tyranny of social media. When a young person is anchored to real friends and family, the vagaries and insults of social media seem far less threatening or significant.

And, of course, no community is more important in this regard than the community of faith, because our churches and synagogues and houses of worship offer a life of meaning and purpose that stands utterly opposed to the arbitrary, angry, and exploitative world of Big Tech. The faith I know best is my own, the Christian faith, with its pattern of worship, confession, repentance, and reconciliation. For the faithful, this pattern is embodied in the church's liturgy, communal gatherings, and holidays that organize the Christian understanding of the seasons and the progress of the year.[2] For many Jews, the Sabbath performs a similar role, challenging the priorities of the always-online age and reorienting the community of faith toward a different pattern of life.[3] In their emphasis on the divine importance of every person, communities of faith are a powerful counterforce to elitist corporate liberalism and shallow social media.

Victory against Big Tech's pathologies requires that we reinvigorate family, neighborhood, school, and church, the places where, in authentic community, we come to know ourselves and one another, exercise our responsibilities, and find our sense of belonging. These are the places where we become citizens, where we become free, where we learn to exercise the sovereignty of a citizen in a free republic. Genuine community is now, more than ever, countercultural—and opposed to the ersatz "global community" pushed by the corrupt and power-hungry Big Tech.

But winning this culture war is, in the end, only part of the fight. To free ourselves from the tyranny of Big Tech, we need a different kind of politics as well—a different kind of political economy. To that effort I now turn.

CHAPTER 11

A NEW POLITICS

Today we are told that the ascendance of Big Tech is inevitable, and so is the economy over which it presides. Globalized, corporatized, consolidated, leveraged for the highly educated and especially those close to data—this is, we are instructed, how it must be. The best that working people can hope for is a check now and again from the government.

The arguments are all very familiar. They are more or less precisely what the corporate barons of the nineteenth century, the J. P. Morgans of the world, proclaimed. And they are as wrong now as they were then. No political economy is inevitable, as the American founders would have reminded us. The sort of society we live in is always a choice. And aristocracy is always unnatural. The founders knew that aristocracy is a political decision, a decision by the upwardly mobile of society to rearrange things for their benefit. The Gilded Age robber barons did this with great success, making corporate liberalism a consensus, bipartisan creed, the default political economy of the establishment. Big Tech has been its greatest beneficiary. But there is no reason we should acquiesce to the corporatists' designs—or control—any longer.

The American founders and successive generations after them had a different idea: that there should be no gradation in social status between capital and labor. Indeed, these earlier Americans expected that every man would occupy "that rank only, which his own industry, or that of his near ancestors, had procured him."[1] For "America," Benjamin Franklin said, "is the land of labor."[2] It would be the common man's republic, where working people governed themselves. And these earlier Americans were confident that if the country's working people—who they expected to constitute the vast majority of the population—received their due, that is, if they were paid the value that their labor created, the working class would be secure and prosperous, America would know no social hierarchy, and the republic would long endure.[3] To that end, they favored an economy of independent producers, domestic manufacturing, and protections for the wages of free labor. This was their republicanism, their political economy of the common man. This was the vision that animated Theodore Roosevelt and propelled him into battle against the trusts. It is a vision worth recovering.

There can be no question, of course, of returning to an earlier era or reconstructing a bygone age. That's not the point. The point is what these earlier Americans thought was the purpose of a republican political economy. It was to promote the interests of the common person, to protect his liberty. To recover that focus, we must confront the plutocracy of our day, Big Tech. And that means we must make a series of different political choices.

Tech has grown powerful, as the earlier robber barons did, with the helping hand of government. Today's Big Tech barons have benefited from lax antitrust enforcement and outdated antitrust laws, from cozy relationships with supposed regulators, and from special protections in the law. All this must end. Our antitrust laws must be updated to challenge today's monopolies. Our enforcement agencies must be overhauled. And the special protections for Big Tech must be abolished.

But these measures alone will not be enough. Challenging Big Tech's power also means challenging the business model of addiction they have used to build their dominance. We must return control over the people's personal data, their property, to the people. We must free ordinary Americans from the constant surveillance and manipulation of the tech giants.

Two further lines of effort are needed. We must stop the Big Tech monopolies' efforts at censorship and information control by giving new power to individuals to challenge Big Tech's information stranglehold. And we must curb the worst abuses of social media, particularly those that target the young.

Taken together, these policies can form a new platform against plutocracy, a program to help restore the common person's republic. And it's a practical program that we can enact now.

■ ■ ■

The ideas that animated Theodore Roosevelt's antitrust movement were distinctly populist and republican, rooted in the American tradition. Decades before, Alexis de Tocqueville had written that nothing had struck him "more forcibly" during his travels in 1830s America "than the general equality of condition among the people."[4] This was a distinguishing feature of American social and economic life, and the point of antitrust legislation was to keep it that way. Antitrust advocates wanted to protect the rights of the small farmer and merchant from predatory practices by larger outfits. They saw this as essential to protecting the ordinary citizen's economic independence. And this economic independence, in turn, was essential to the power to participate in self-government and exert some control over the life of the nation. Antitrust advocates despised concentrated power and saw *economic* concentration no less than the political kind as a profound threat to the authority and standing of the common person. The antitrust movement was built on republican premises from start to finish.[5]

But in recent years it has been under-used and under-appreciated, as both Left and Right made their peace with bigness. After years of courts' treating antitrust law as merely a question of whether consumer prices have increased, the whole doctrine is ripe for a rediscovery of its populist, republican roots. And in the fight for antitrust enforcement against Big Tech, it could find them.

Remember the market abuses of Google. The company controls upwards of 90 percent of the market for online searches, both in America and globally. Investigators at the European Union have amassed evidence that Google has systematically used that market dominance to favor its own platforms—Google Travel, Google Shopping—over those of its rivals.[6] That's a fit subject for antitrust enforcement. Then there's Google's dominance of digital advertising. Over the course of a decade, Google has purchased and built dominant shares in every level of the online advertising market, on both the buyer *and* seller sides.[7] Google even owns the advertising exchanges, the digital auction in which advertising space is bought and sold electronically in a near-instantaneous bidding process. Google's systematic acquisition of every layer of the advertising market may itself constitute a violation of the Clayton and Sherman Antitrust Acts.

And all that is before we get to Google-owned YouTube. Advertisers pay a king's ransom to get their digital ads on YouTube, and then, according to the platform's customers and competitors, YouTube insists that these advertisers promise to use Google ad services to place ads on *other* sites. That's what's known in the antitrust world as "tying," the practice of conditioning the sale of one product to the purchase of a separate product, the most famous example being Microsoft's effort to tie its Internet Explorer web browser to its Windows operating system in the 1990s, which a court ruled illegal.[8] Google has allegedly tied access to ad space on Google Search in the same way, leveraging its dominance in both video and online search to create dominance in a third market, advertising.[9] That, too, is a ripe target for antitrust enforcement.

Or consider Facebook. As we have seen, 99 percent of American adults who use social media use Facebook, some 210 million Americans, a degree of market power that isn't so much concentration as it is complete and utter dominance.[10] Facebook dominates users' time, as well. The platform captures 83 percent of consumers' time spent on social media sites, dwarf-ing the competition.[11] Facebook attained all that market power by repeat-edly promising to guard users' privacy, in contrast to its principal early competitor, MySpace.[12] But once MySpace was vanquished as a rival, Facebook eagerly launched into the very surveillance of its customers it had loudly promised to abjure, and all without customers' knowledge or consent. In short, Facebook bested its primary opponent by deliberately misleading the public about its own business practices. That, some anti-trust scholars argue, is exactly the sort of deceptive conduct in support of a monopoly that the Sherman Act forbids.[13]

And the harm to consumers is quite real. Facebook's services are nominally free, but in actual fact the constant, prying surveillance Face-book inflicts on its customers is a form of "monopoly rent"—an extrac-tion of value—consumers don't want to pay but are powerless to refuse. And that in turn indicates just how little real competition Facebook faces. As one scholar put it, "The tendency is to think that Facebook's free service reflects consumer surplus, yet nearly every advertising market in the U.S. is in decline as American consumers indicate a preference for ad-free communications and media. In the world of television and video, consumers have flocked from ad-supported TV to ad-free" competitors, like Netflix and Prime Video.[14] But not in the world of social media. There Facebook reigns, because Facebook is the only real choice. Simi-larly, consumers tell researchers over and again that they value digital privacy, and yet Facebook maintains dominant market share with inces-sant monitoring because Facebook is the only real choice.[15]

It's not as if Facebook customers love Facebook. The American Customer Satisfaction Index (ACSI) reports that social media has one of the lowest scores of all the industries it tracks. "With an industry average of 72, social media's ASCI [*sic*] score is lower than even health insurance and airlines."[16] Facebook meanwhile earns a score of 67, which is, for comparison purposes, not only lower than the social media average, but lower than almost every single American airline currently flying.[17] Why do customers continue to use a social media platform they find middling at best, that pushes ads they don't want to see, that violates their privacy in ways they do not approve? Because they have no real choice. That is what monopoly looks like.[18]

Both Google and Facebook are ripe targets for antitrust enforcement—and breakup. At a minimum, Google should be forced to give up YouTube as well as its control of the digital advertising market. Facebook should lose Instagram and WhatsApp, purchases it made with the purpose of forestalling competition. And Congress should impose new rules on what else the giant tech companies and similar corporate behemoths can own. The Big Tech platforms have grown to leviathans not only by snapping up the competition or running them out of business, but also by consolidating formerly independent companies across different industries under one giant corporate superstructure, a model pioneered, once again, by last century's robber barons. It is time to stop it once and for all.

Google's parent company, Alphabet Inc., is a case study. Alphabet not only owns and runs Google, its original, core business, but now also controls a panoply of other businesses in other industries. For example, as scholar Michael Lind has catalogued, Google owns "YouTube, the world's largest video-sharing site; a smartphone division with Android and Pixel phones; Waymo, a self-driving car project; Project Wing, a commercial drone delivery service; Google Fiber, a high-speed internet, TV, and phone service that competes with cable companies; Google Cloud, a cloud-computing platform; G Suite, which includes Gmail, Calendar, and Hangouts; Verily, a health care company; Sidewalk Labs, an urban development company; Google Capital, a 'growth equity investment fund'; DeepMind, which focuses on artificial intelligence (AI); Project Loon, which seeks to use hot-air balloons to expand global internet access; Jacquard, which makes smart fabric; Soli, which uses radar for touchless gesture control; and Spotlight Stories, which makes virtual reality films."[19]

And it's not just Alphabet and Google. Amazon is famous as an online retailer, but it also owns Amazon Web Services, a cloud-computing company that looks to become Amazon's major source of revenue in the decades ahead—and was the means by which Amazon effectively destroyed the social media company Parler (by denying it cloud access). Amazon also owns a video game streaming site, a satellite company, and an online health information service. Facebook, meanwhile, owns Libra, a digital currency, in addition to Instagram and WhatsApp.[20]

Economists argue whether *horizontal* mergers, which consolidate several competing firms from the same industry into one giant operation, or *vertical* mergers, which put an entire supply chain under one company's control, are efficient. What they generally agree on is that conglomerate mergers, the kind of reach-your-tentacles-into-every-conceivable-market mergers that Alphabet and Amazon and Facebook have each pursued, are not.[21] Congress should ban them.

In the 1930s, the Glass-Steagall Act divided commercial from investment banking, a kind of ban on conglomerate mergers in the financial world (which Congress partly repealed, unwisely, in 1999). Now we need a Glass-Steagall Act for Big Tech. Congress should force tech companies to choose: act as consumer-facing digital platforms *or* become producers of goods and services. Big Tech ought not be permitted to do all of the above all at once. A new Glass-Steagall Act for the tech sector would halt tech's march into every industry in America and circumscribe its dominance over American life.

There are other antitrust changes Congress can and should make. Congress should crack down on mergers involving digital platforms by giving the Department of Justice the power to designate major tech firms as "dominant"; those "dominant" firms should then be prevented from merging with or acquiring another business, whatever that business may be. This proposal would emphatically apply to the dominant platforms of Amazon, Facebook, Apple, Twitter, and Google. In fact, Congress should toughen merger rules across the board, for all corporate conglomerates, by strengthening the presumption that mergers that result in substantial market share are illegal and by making clear that all mergers, including "vertical" mergers, must undergo rigorous antitrust scrutiny.

And while Congress is augmenting the antitrust laws, it should do more to improve antitrust enforcement. For decades, enforcement authority has been divided between the Department of Justice and the Federal Trade Commission. As the crowning achievement of Woodrow Wilson's corporatist settlement, the FTC is nominally independent, its law enforcement efforts mostly lax, and its relationship with industry remarkably cozy. Big Tech in particular has long since figured out how to get the FTC's revolving door of regulators to revolve in its favor.

Congress can change that with legislation toughening antitrust enforcement. First, stop the turf wars between the Department of Justice and the FTC by giving enforcement authority clearly and fully to the Department of Justice. The Department of Justice has an entire division devoted to antitrust. The Department of Justice should have unequivocal authority to enforce the law. Unlike the FTC, the Department of Justice can be held politically accountable *by voters*, the people who are supposed to run this country through their elected representatives. As for the FTC, it should be overhauled from top to bottom. Congress should place the FTC under the direction of the Department of Justice and charge the commission with developing economic and market analysis to support and guide the department's antitrust enforcement activities. The FTC should also be given broader regulatory enforcement power over data privacy, again subject to Department of Justice oversight.

Antitrust has become a legal backwater in recent decades. But the curse of bigness is back, and antitrust enforcement must come back with it, updated to perform its original, republican function: protecting the independence of the American people from oligarchic control.

■ ■ ■

Antitrust legislation and enforcement on its own, however, will not suffice to defeat the tyranny of Big Tech. Unwinding mergers can only go so far in the grand scheme. Even a shrunken Facebook remains dangerous precisely to the extent it can continue to control Americans' time and attention, and precisely insofar as it can scoop up Americans' personal data—their personal *property*—without limit or consent. More must be done to strike at this, the heart of Big Tech's power, which lies in its business model of addiction.

Big Tech runs, let us not forget, on advertising. It is because the big platforms want to sell Americans' attention to advertisers that they devise increasingly manipulative and invasive means of getting our attention to begin with. It is because they want their advertisements to be viewed, to be effective, to lead to sales, that they gather increasingly voluminous amounts of data on their users—us—building individual profiles worthy of the Orwellian imagination. Addiction for the purpose of advertising is the business of Big Tech.

So we must strike at that business in order to limit the power of the tech class. Big Tech's danger to the common man, which is to say, its danger to the *republic*, is not merely its size but its endless degrading of the ordinary citizen's independence and control over his own life. To stop that degradation, we must stop Big Tech's spying, its appropriation of individual property, and its shameless manipulation of its users. To that end: I propose ending the Section 230 immunity from suit for any tech corporation that engages in manipulative, behavioral advertising. That's the type of advertising premised on individual user data, with ads keyed to individual characteristics and designed to leverage personal preferences to influence the user toward a sale. Behavioral ads only work with reams of personal data, which gives the tech platforms incentive to go and acquire it. This proposal would change that.

It's a simple proposition. Engage in behavioral advertising, lose the Section 230 shield. Manipulative advertising based on personal characteristics is far from the passive distribution of third-party content Congress envisaged when it adopted Section 230 a quarter century ago. And behavioral ads drive many of tech platforms' worst pathologies—the surveillance, the addiction race, the data pilfering. But Section 230's shield from liability is worth far more to Big Tech than even behavioral advertising. Section 230 is the giant government subsidy on which Big

Tech feeds and has built its empire. It's what Big Tech believes it cannot live without. And that's exactly why Congress should deny it to all tech platforms that accept or promote or engage in behavioral advertising—or that provide personal data that the platform knows will be used for behavioral ads to third parties. The federal government should stop subsidizing the surveillance and manipulation of American citizens.

Follow that up with this: give every American the right to stop data collection altogether with the click of a button. That's what I call the Do Not Track proposal, legislation I introduced in the Senate. Ending Section 230 immunity for behavioral advertising would powerfully discourage tech companies from personal data mining and surveillance; Do Not Track would give citizens the capacity to stop it almost altogether. Some years ago, tech industry groups promoted a "do not track" program to give users control over their personal information. But the effort was voluntary, and, lo and behold, the dominant platforms opted out. Congress should give Do Not Track legal force by giving every American the right to click a button in a web browser, or to download an app, that would prevent the tech platforms from collecting any data beyond what is strictly necessary for a website or app's operation. No more surveillance all across the web, no more tracking and spying—and strict penalties for violation. Users would be able to control their own data. As part of the package, individuals should also be able to request the tech platforms *delete* the personal data they have on file. This is a measure that would put individuals back in control.

Taken together, these proposals strike at the core of the Big Tech business model, the center of tech's influence and control. There is no better way to send power flowing back to the ordinary citizen than to tear down Big Tech's empire of surveillance and manipulation.

■ ■ ■

Big Tech has imposed enormous social costs as the price for its power, often disproportionately on the young. Social media has profoundly changed the way younger Americans communicate with each other, how they relate to each other, form friendships, pursue romance, and entertain themselves—and mostly, it would appear, for the worse. The hallmarks of the tech era include soaring rates of loneliness, bullying, depression, and suicide among young people.

During the previous Gilded Age, reformers rewrote American law to stop the exploitation of children and child labor. Today, we need to protect young people from the worst abuses of Big Tech. Research shows that social media is particularly harmful for the mental health of girls between the ages of ten and fourteen.[22] So we can start by raising the age for opening a social media account from thirteen to sixteen and requiring proof of identity.

Congress should also consider curbing the most egregiously addictive features of social media, which turn every smartphone into a mobile casino for attention. Infinite scroll—a feature first introduced by Facebook to keep users poring over the News Feed, scrolling and scrolling with no end in sight—would be a logical place to start. Google-owned YouTube adopted a similar tactic with Autoplay, the feature, defaulted to "On," that keeps videos loading into the customer's suggestion feed without end. Congress should consider regulation that would bar these features outright, or at least default them to "Off." And policy-makers should additionally consider pushing the social media giants to set default time limits for app usage—say, an hour a day—that users could adjust, but only by making a conscious decision. The aim of these proposals is, in the end, to put customers (and parents) more firmly in control of their (and their children's) experience online, and to lessen Big Tech's manipulative power.

■ ■ ■

Finally, there is the question of Big Tech's control over information, journalism, news, and censorship. Facebook's cofounder, Chris Hughes, said it himself in the starkest terms: "The most problematic aspect of

Facebook's power is Mark [Zuckerberg]'s unilateral control over speech. There is no precedent for his ability to monitor, organize and even censor the conversations of two billion people."[23] Make it three billion, and counting.

The simplest, most direct solution to this quandary is also the best, and it involves once again Section 230. That law grants Big Tech privileges not enjoyed by any other publisher or editor in America, and yet thanks in no small measure to the Section 230 subsidy, the Big Tech platforms are now the largest publishers on the planet. So, treat the tech companies like the publishers they truly are, and let individuals sue them for acts of censorship or other breaches of good faith.

It would work like this. At present, the tech companies issue terms of service to every user who gets online, but they are almost entirely unenforceable, seeing as how Section 230 prevents most lawsuits. Congress should adopt legislation making those terms of service *binding*, actually enforceable, and further require that the tech companies apply the terms of service fairly, without political bias or discrimination. Congress should also give individuals a cause of action to get into court if tech reneges and violates its own terms. If the platform loses the suit, it would owe $5000 for every violation of the service terms, plus the attorneys' fees for each user who prevails.

That would change the game. That would make the tech platforms accountable, finally, for the censorship they always insist doesn't occur and for which they can never be punished. And it would do it in a time-honored American manner, by letting the American citizen have her or his day in court. To be clear, this isn't government imposing new rules from the outside. This is government making Big Tech's own rules, its own service terms and conditions, actually enforceable, and returning rightful power to the average American.

■ ■ ■

These reforms are only a beginning, of course—but they are a necessary beginning. I urge their adoption not because new laws can solve every problem, but because Congress has a duty to defend our republican way of life; it has a constitutional responsibility to "promote the general welfare," the common good for the common people of this nation upon whom our system of self-government rests. "Self-government," Theodore Roosevelt once said, "is not an easy thing. Only those communities are fit for it in which the average individual practices the virtue of self-command, of self-restraint, of wise disinterestedness."[24] Roosevelt's politics were an effort to make it possible for the "average individual," the ordinary man and woman, to acquire that kind of independence and turn it into political control. "[W]e had come to the stage where for our people what was needed was real democracy," he later said—real control by the ordinary, everyday, working people of the nation.[25]

Corporate liberalism, oligarchy, rule by the elite—these need not be our destiny. The tyranny of Big Tech *can* be challenged. We can forge a better political economy, one in keeping with our history and our highest aspirations. Theodore Roosevelt understood that our republic was a republic of the common person. This is what made it a republic of liberty. Now we must recall his example and make it so again.

ACKNOWLEDGMENTS

Any thanks must begin with my wife, Erin, not least because this book began in conversation with her, and she was the one who first encouraged me to write it. She has read more versions of the manuscript than I dare count, and provided feedback and insight that was ever timely and incisive. She is the love of my life and the partner without whom I can't imagine doing anything that I do. This book is dedicated to her. I'd like to thank Tom Spence and his terrific team at Regnery who had the courage to stand up to the cancel mob when others wouldn't. Because of his bravery, this book came to print. Harry Crocker and Kathleen Curran at Regnery were the consummate professionals, and it was a true pleasure working with them. Thanks to Chris Weihs and Pierson Furnish, who provided top-notch research help at various stages of the project, and a special thanks to Jacob Reses, who has been my one-of-a-kind blue-sky thinker, creative sounding board, and researcher par excellence. This book would not be what it is without him. And thanks finally to the many family and friends who listened, read, prayed, and encouraged along the way. I'm grateful for all of you.

NOTES

CHAPTER 1: THE RETURN OF THE MONOPOLIES

1. "Senators Hawley and Markey Introduce Bipartisan Legislation to Stop Internet Companies from Spying on Children," announcement by office of Senator Josh Hawley, March 12, 2019, https://www.hawley.senate.gov/senators-hawley-and-markey-introduce-bipartisan-legislation-stop-internet-companies-spying-children.

2. "Sen. Hawley Introduces Legislation to Curb Social Media Addiction," announcement by office of Senator Josh Hawley, July 30, 2019, https://www.hawley.senate.gov/sen-hawley-introduces-legislation-curb-social-media-addiction; "Senator Hawley Introduces Legislation to Amend Section 230 Immunity for Big Tech Companies," announcement by office of Senator Josh Hawley, June 19, 2019, https://www.hawley.senate.gov/senator-hawley-introduces-legislation-amend-section-230-immunity-big-tech-companies.

3. Jack Suntrup, "Hawley Launches Investigation into Facebook as Fallout over User Data Continues," *St. Louis Post-Dispatch*, April 2, 2018, https://www.stltoday.com/news/local/govt-and-politics/hawley-launches-investigation-into-facebook-as-fallout-over-user-data-continues/article_e532e72f-b744-5c6f-9990-9737774d206f.html; Timothy B. Lee, "Why Google Should Be Afraid of a Missouri Republican's Google Probe," Ars

Technica, November 14, 2017, https://arstechnica.com/tech-policy/2017/11/conservative-backlash-a-missouri-republican-is-investigating-google/.

4. See, e.g., Martin J. Sklar, "Woodrow Wilson and the Political Economy of Modern United States Liberalism," *Studies on the Left* (Fall 1960); James Weinstein, "An Obituary for the Progressive Movement," *American Quarterly* 22 (Spring 1970), 26; James Weinstein, *The Corporate Ideal in the Liberal State, 1900–1918* (Boston: Beacon, 1968).

5. "Social Media Fact Sheet," Pew Research Center, June 12, 2019, https://www.pewresearch.org/internet/fact-sheet/social-media/. See similar analysis based on older figures in Dina Srinivasan, "The Antitrust Case against Facebook: A Monopolist's Journey towards Pervasive Surveillance in Spite of Consumers' Preference for Privacy," *Berkeley Business Law Journal* 16, no. 1 (2019): 39–101, https://lawcat.berkeley.edu/record/1128876?ln=en, 84.

6. Mathew Ingram, "The Facebook Armageddon," *Columbia Journalism Review* (Winter 2018), https://www.cjr.org/special_report/facebook-media-buzzfeed.php.

7. "Search Engine Market Share United States of America," Statcounter, https://gs.statcounter.com/search-engine-market-share/all/united-states-of-america.

8. "Desktop Browser Market Share Worldwide," Statcounter, https://gs.statcounter.com/browser-market-share/desktop/worldwide; "Mobile Browser Market Share Worldwide," Statcounter, https://gs.statcounter.com/browser-market-share/mobile/worldwide.

9. "Smartphone Market Share," IDC, September 14, 2020, https://www.idc.com/promo/smartphone-market-share/os.

10. Riley Panko, "The Popularity of Google Maps: Trends in Navigation Apps in 2018," The Manifest, July 10, 2018, https://themanifest.com/mobile-apps/popularity-google-maps-trends-navigation-apps-2018.

11. Paul Briggs, "Global Twitter Users 2019," Emarketer, December 12, 2019, https://www.emarketer.com/content/global-twitter-users-2019.

12. Figure estimated by Consumer Intelligence Research Partners. See Fareeha Ali, "Amazon Prime Has 126 Million Members in the US," Digital Commerce 360, October 26, 2020, https://www.digitalcommerce360.com/article/amazon-prime-membership/.

13. Pippa Stevens, "This Breakdown of Retail Sales Shows Why Amazon Is Leading the Stock Market," CNBC, May 15, 2020, https://www.cnbc.com/2020/05/15/this-breakdown-of-retail-sales-data-shows-why-amazon-is-leading-the-stock-market.html.

14. Kif Leswing, "Apple Says Consumers and Advertisers Spent More Than $500 Billion through Apps Last Year," CNBC, June 15, 2020, https://www. cnbc.com/2020/06/15/apple-consumers-advertisers-spent-519-billion-through-apps-in-2019.html.

15. "Lord of the Rings, 2020 and Stuffed Oreos: Read the Andrew Bosworth Memo," *New York Times,* January 7, 2020, https://www.nytimes. com/2020/01/07/technology/facebook-andrew-bosworth-memo.html.

16. Ibid.

17. Robert Epstein, "Why Google Poses a Serious Threat to Democracy, and How to End That Threat," testimony before the U.S. Senate Judiciary Subcommittee on the Constitution, June 16, 2019, https://www.judiciary. senate.gov/download/epstein-testimony.

18. "Facebook Settles FTC Charges That It Deceived Consumers by Failing to Keep Privacy Promises," Federal Trade Commission, November 29, 2011, https://www.ftc.gov/news-events/press-releases/2011/11/ facebook-settles-ftc-charges-it-deceived-consumers-failing-keep.

19. "FTC Imposes $5 Billion Penalty and Sweeping New Privacy Restrictions on Facebook," Federal Trade Commission, July 24, 2019, https://www.ftc.gov/ news-events/press-releases/2019/07/ ftc-imposes-5-billion-penalty-sweeping-new-privacy-restrictions.

20. "Antitrust: Commission Fines Google €1.49 Billion for Abusive Practices in Online Advertising," European Commission, March 20, 2019, https:// ec.europa.eu/commission/presscorner/detail/en/IP_19_1770.

21. "Antitrust: Commission Fines Google €2.42 Billion for Abusing Dominance as Search Engine by Giving Illegal Advantage to Own Comparison Shopping Service," European Commission, June 27, 2017, https://ec.europa. eu/commission/presscorner/detail/en/IP_17_1784; "Antitrust: Commission Fines Google €4.34 Billion for Illegal Practices Regarding Android Mobile Devices to Strengthen Dominance of Google's Search Engine," European Commission, July 18, 2018, https://ec.europa.eu/commission/presscorner/ detail/en/IP_18_4581.

22. For dollar equivalent of euro total at the time of the third fine's announcement see James Vincent, "Google Hit with €1.5 Billion Antitrust Fine by EU," The Verge, March 20, 2019, https://www.theverge. com/2019/3/20/18270891/google-eu-antitrust-fine-adsense-advertising.

23. "Antitrust: Commission Sends Statement of Objections to Amazon for the Use of Non-Public Independent Seller Data and Opens Second Investigation into Its E-Commerce Business Practices," European Commission,

November 10, 2020, https://ec.europa.eu/commission/presscorner/detail/en/ip_20_2077.

24. "Justice Department Sues Monopolist Google for Violating Antitrust Laws," Department of Justice, October 20, 2020, https://www.justice.gov/opa/pr/justice-department-sues-monopolist-google-violating-antitrust-laws.

CHAPTER 2: THE ROBBER BARONS

1. See H. W. Brands, *T. R.: The Last Romantic* (New York: Basic Books, 1997), 436–37.

2. "Notes and News: Northern Securities Company," *The Railway Age,* February 21, 1902. See also Ron Chernow, *The House of Morgan: An American Banking Dynasty and the Rise of Modern Finance* (New York: Grove Press, 1990), 242.

3. For an introduction to Morgan the financier, see, e.g., Ron Chernow, *The House of Morgan: An American Banking Dynasty and the Rise of Modern Finance* (New York: Grove Press, 1990). See also Michael Hiltzik, *Iron Empires: Robber Barons, Railroads and the Making of Modern America* (New York: Houghton Mifflin, 2020), 39–54.

4. See "City Isolated by Ravages of Storm," *Washington Times*, February 22, 1902.

5. There is some recent dispute over the dates of Morgan's meeting with Roosevelt. I have here followed the standard account; see, e.g., Edmund Morris, *Theodore Rex* (New York: Random House, 2001), 91–92. But for a recent account arguing the Morgan-Roosevelt meeting actually occurred on Sunday, February 23, see Susan Berfield, *The Hour of Fate: Theodore Roosevelt, J. P. Morgan, and the Battle to Transform American Capitalism* (New York: Bloomsbury Publishing, 2020), 118–19. Berfield draws in part on an earlier account whose chronology differs somewhat, Henry F. Pringle, *Theodore Roosevelt: A Biography* (New York: Harcourt, Brace and Company, 1931), 256.

6. See Martin J. Sklar, *The Corporate Reconstruction of American Capitalism, 1890–1916* (Cambridge: Cambridge University Press, 1988), 1–32.

7. See, e.g., Charles Postel, *The Populist Vision* (New York: Oxford University Press, 2007), 137–71; Jack Beatty, *Age of Betrayal: The Triumph of Money in America, 1865–1900* (New York: Vintage, 2007), 301–45.

8. Alfred D. Chandler Jr., "The Railroads: The First Modern Business Enterprises, 1850s–1860s," in *Colossus: How the Corporation Changed America*, ed. Jack Beatty (New York: Broadway Books, 2001), 83.

9. Chandler, "The Railroads," 88.

10. See John A. Garraty, *The New Commonwealth, 1877–1890* (New York: Harper, 1968), 85.

11. Quoted in Beatty, *Age of Betrayal*, 14.

12. Beatty, *Age of Betrayal*, 14.

13. Chandler, "The Railroads," 90.

14. Chandler, "The Railroads," 90; Beatty, *Age of Betrayal*, 14.

15. Chandler, "The Railroads," 91–94.

16. Beatty, *Age of Betrayal*, 15.

17. Hiltzik, *Iron Empires*, xiii; Beatty, *Age of Betrayal*, 15.

18. Beatty, *Age of Betrayal*, 15.

19. Chandler, "The Railroads," 94.

20. Beatty, *Age of Betrayal*, 15–16.

21. Hiltzik, *Iron Empires*, 3-21, 101.

22. Ibid., 43.

23. Beatty, *Age of Betrayal*, 232–34.

24. "How I Was Converted—Politically: By a Kansas Progressive Republican," *The Outlook* 96 (December 17, 1910): 857–58.

25. Peter H. Argersinger, *Populism and Politics: William Alfred Peffer and the People's Party* (Lexington, Kentucky: University of Kentcky Press, 1974), 4, 7.

26. Hallie Farmer, "The Economic Background of Frontier Populism," *Mississippi Valley Historical Review* 10, no. 4 (1924): 406–427, https://academic.oup.com/jah/article/10/4/406/700213.

27. William C. Reuter, "Business Journals and Gilded Age Politics," *The Historian* 56, no. 1 (Autumn 1993), 55.

28. Hiltzik, *Iron Empires*, 59–65.

29. Ibid. See also Jay Boyd Crawford, *The Credit Mobilier of America: Its Origin and History* (Boston: C. W. Calkins & Co., 1880).

30. *Report of the Select Committee to Investigate the Alleged Crédit Mobiler Bribery, Made to the House of Representative February 18, 1873* (Washington, D.C.: U.S. Government Printing Office, 1873), x.

31. Beatty, *Age of Betrayal*, 192–93.

32. See Hiltzik, *Iron Empires*, 219-220.

33. Beatty, *Age of Betrayal*, 192–93.

34. Hiltzik, *Iron Empires*, 162.

35. Thomas G. Sherman, *The Forum*, November 1889, 273.

36. See Hiltzik, *Iron Empires*, 335–38.

37. See Chernow, *The House of Morgan*, 93–105.

38. Hiltzik, *Iron Empires*, 178.
39. Ibid., 172.
40. Sklar, *The Corporate Reconstruction of American Capitalism*, 165.
41. Hiltzik, *Iron Empires*, 209–10.
42. Beatty, *Age of Betrayal*, 385.
43. Naomi R. Lamoreaux, *The Great Merger Movement in American Business, 1895–1904* (New York: Cambridge University Press, 1985), 1–2.
44. Hiltzik, *Iron Empires*, 207.
45. Jeremiah Whipple Jenks, *The Trust Problem* (New York: McClure, Phillips & Co., 1900), 36 (emphasis added).
46. Quoted in James L. Huston, "The American Revolutionaries, the Political Economy of Aristocracy, and the American Concept of the Distribution of Wealth, 1765–1900," *American Historical Review* (October 1993), 1079.
47. Ibid.
48. Beatty, *Age of Betrayal*, 11–13. See also "Incorporating the Republic: The Corporation in Antebellum Political Culture," *Harvard Law Review* 102 (1989): 1890–1897.
49. *Liggett Co. v. Lee*, 288 U.S. 517, 549 (1933).
50. Beatty, *Age of Betrayal*, 13.

CHAPTER 3: THE LAST REPUBLICAN

1. Edmund Morris, *Theodore Rex* (New York: Random House, 2001), 91–92. See also Joseph Bucklin Bishop, *Theodore Roosevelt and His Time: Shown in His Own Letters*, volume 1 (New York: Charles Scribner's Sons, 1920), 184.
2. See Kathleen Dalton, *Theodore Roosevelt: A Strenuous Life* (New York: Vintage Books, 2002), 169.
3. Theodore Roosevelt, *An Autobiography* (New York: Da Capo Press, 1985), 439.
4. For a summary, see Martin J. Sklar, *The Corporate Reconstruction of American Capitalism, 1890–1916* (Cambridge, Massachusetts: Cambridge University Press, 1988), 306–8, 339–64.
5. Theodore Roosevelt, "Limitation of Government Power," in *Progressive Principles*, ed. by Wilmer H. Youngman (London: Effingham Wilson, 1913), 213.
6. Theodore Roosevelt, "The New Nationalism," in *The Works of Theodore Roosevelt: Social Justice and Popular Rule: Essays, Addresses, and Public Statements Relating to the Progressive Movement, 1910–1916*, volume 19 (New York: Arno Press, 1974), 14–15.

7. See Quentin Skinner, "The Idea of Negative Liberty: Machiavellian and Modern Perspectives," in *Visions of Politics*, volume 2 (Cambridge, Massachusetts: Cambridge University Press, 2002), 197.

8. Theodore Roosevelt, Oration in Dakota Territory, July 4, 1886, Theodore Roosevelt Digital Library, Dickinson State University.

9. For an assessment of the prevalence of this theme in American politics in the middle nineteenth century, see Marvin Meyers, *The Jacksonian Persuasion: Politics and Belief* (Stanford, California: Stanford University Press, 1957), 16–56.

10. Roosevelt, "The New Nationalism," 15.

11. Ibid., 29.

12. See, e.g., Quentin Skinner, "The Idea of Negative Liberty," 196–210. For a discussion of the American reception of republican themes, see J. G. A. Pocock, *The Machiavellian Moment: Florentine Political Thought and the Atlantic Republican Tradition* (Princeton, New Jersey: Princeton University Press, 1975), 506–52.

13. See, e.g., Joshua Hawley, *Theodore Roosevelt: Preacher of Righteousness* (New Haven, Connecticut: Yale University Press, 2008), 138–41.

14. See Tom Holland, *Rubicon: The Last Years of the Roman Republic* (New York: Anchor Books, 2003), 338–78.

15. See Skinner, "Classical Liberty, Renaissance Translation and the English Civil War," in *Visions of Politics*, 312–18.

16. For an analysis of the Roman (and neo-roman) view of liberty, see Quentin Skinner, *Liberty before Liberalism* (Cambridge: Cambridge University Press, 1998), 1–99. See also Skinner, "Classical Liberty," 312–18.

17. See Skinner, "Classical Liberty," 312–18.

18. For an exploration of this view, see Larry Siedentop, *Inventing the Individual: The Origins of Western Liberalism* (Cambridge, Massachusetts: Harvard Belknap Press, 2014), 7–47.

19. Siedentop, *Inventing the Individual*, 353.

20. Ibid., 59–66.

21. 1 Cor. 6:19 (NIV).

22. 1 Cor. 1:26 (NIV).

23. 1 Cor. 1:27 (NIV).

24. Galatians 3:28 (ESV).

25. See Siedentop, *Inventing the Individual*, 61–63.

26. For more on this development, see Charles Taylor, *Sources of the Self: The Making of Modern Identity* (Cambridge, Massachusetts: Harvard University Press, 1989), 211–33.

27. For the influence of Harrington and company on the early Americans, see Bernard Bailyn, *The Ideological Origins of the American Revolution* (Cambridge, Massachusetts: Harvard Belknap Press, 1967), 34–54. For more on the prominence of the agrarian yeoman in English revolutionary thought and the American reception, see Pocock, *The Machiavellian Moment*, 506–52.

28. Thomas Jefferson letter to John Jay, August 23, 1785.

29. See Jack Rakove, *Original Meanings* (New York: Knopf, 1997), 42–43.

30. Sklar, *The Corporate Reconstruction of American Capitalism*, 184–88.

31. Roosevelt, "The New Nationalism," 17.

32. Sklar, *The Corporate Reconstruction of American Capitalism*, 202–3.

33. This was the so-called Foulke plan, developed by William Dudley Foulke in consultation with Roosevelt. Sklar, *The Corporate Reconstruction of American Capitalism*, 306–8.

34. Ibid., 359.

35. Ibid., 356.

CHAPTER 4: THE TRIUMPH OF CORPORATE LIBERALISM

1. Woodrow Wilson, *The State: Elements of Practical and Historical Politics* (Boston: D.C. Heath and Company, 1893), 646–47, 666.

2. Woodrow Wilson, "What Jefferson Would Do," *The Public Papers of Woodrow Wilson* [PPWW], ed. by Ray Stannard Baker and William E. Dodd, volume 2 (New York: Harper & Brothers, 1925–27), 424.

3. Martin J. Sklar, *The Corporate Reconstruction of American Capitalism*, 402.

4. Wilson, "Issues of Freedom," *PPWW* 2, 285.

5. Wilson, *The New Freedom: A Call for the Emancipation of the Generous Energies of a People* (New York: Doubleday, Page & Company, 1913), 5.

6. Wilson, "Bankers and Statesmanship," *PPWW* 2, 229 (emphasis added).

7. Wilson, "The Tariff and the Trusts," *PPWW* 2, 411.

8. Wilson, "The Lawyer and the Community," *PPWW* 2, 256.

9. See, e.g., John Milton Cooper, *The Warrior and the Priest: Woodrow Wilson and Theodore Roosevelt* (Cambridge, Massachusetts: Harvard Belknap Press, 1983), 212–14; Alan L. Seltzer, "Woodrow Wilson as 'Corporate-Liberal': Toward a Reconstruction of Left Revisionist Historiography," *The Western Political Quarterly* 30 (June 1977): 183–212.

10. See Cooper, *The Warrior and the Priest*, 212–13.

11. Wilson, "Speech of Acceptance," *PPWW* 2, 464.

12. Wilson, *The New Freedom*, 164–65.
13. Wilson, "The Puritan," *PPWW* 1, 365.
14. Wilson, "Richmond Address," *PPWW* 2, 377.
15. Ibid., 376.
16. For more on Wilson's religious background and its implications for his politics, see Alan L. Seltzer, "Woodrow Wilson as 'Corporate-Liberal,'" 191–93.
17. See Merle Curti, "Woodrow Wilson's Conception of Human Nature," *Midwest Journal of Political Science* 1, no. 1 (May 1957), 4–6, 13; John Morton Blum, *Woodrow Wilson and the Politics of Morality* (Boston: Little, Brown & Company, 1956), 5–13.
18. Wilson, *The State*, 661.
19. Ibid., 633.
20. Quoted in Seltzer, "Woodrow Wilson as 'Corporate-Liberal,'" 192.
21. Wilson, *The State*, 647.
22. Wilson, "Richmond Address," *PPWW* 2, 372–73.
23. Wilson, "The Puritan," *PPWW* 1, 366.
24. Wilson, *The New Freedom*, 5.
25. Wilson, *The State*, 647.
26. Wilson, "The Lawyer and the Community," *PPWW* 2, 258.
27. Wilson, "The Puritan," *PPWW* 1, 366.
28. Walter Lippmann, *The Phantom Public* (New York: Harcourt, Brace and Company, 1925), 105.
29. Walter Lippmann, *Public Opinion* (New York: Harcourt, Brace and Company, 1922), 272.
30. See James L. Huston, "The American Revolutionaries, the Political Economy of Aristocracy, and the American Concept of the Distribution of Wealth, 1765–1900," *American Historical Review* (October 1993), 1083.
31. Blum, *Woodrow Wilson and the Politics of Morality*, 5–13.
32. See Sklar, *The Corporate Reconstruction of American Capitalism*, 4–40.
33. See Huston, "The American Revolutionaries," 1082–83; Marvin Meyers, *The Jacksonian Persuasion: Politics and Belief* (Stanford, California: Stanford University Press, 1957), 18-24.
34. I am indebted to Christopher Lasch for identifying the significance of this speech and for his analysis. See Christopher Lasch, *Revolt of the Elites and the Betrayal of Democracy* (New York: W. W. Norton & Co., 1996), 74–76.
35. James Bryant Conant, "Education for a Classless Society: The Jeffersonian Tradition," *The Atlantic*, May 1940.
36. Lasch, *Revolt of the Elites*, 76.

37. Wilson, "Labor Day Speech" in *A Crossroads of Freedom: The 1912 Campaign Speeches of Woodrow Wilson*, ed. John Wells Davidson (New Haven, Connecticut: Yale University Press, 1956), 79.

38. Sklar, *The Corporate Reconstruction of American Capitalism*, 420–22.

39. See *Standard Oil v. United States*, 221 U.S. 1 (1911).

40. Sklar, *The Corporate Reconstruction of American Capitalism*, 420.

41. Ibid., 423.

42. Ibid.

43. See David M. Kennedy, *Freedom from Fear: The American People in Depression and War, 1929–1945* (New York: Oxford University Press, 1999), 359; Cooper, *Warrior and the Priest*, 353. See also Matt Stoller, *Goliath: The 100-Year War between Monopoly Power and Populism* (New York: Simon & Schuster, 2019), 118–47.

CHAPTER 5: ADDICTING AMERICA

1. Facebook, Inc., Form S-1 Registration Statement, United States Securities and Exchange Commission archives, February 1, 2012, https://www.sec.gov/Archives/edgar/data/1326801/000119312512034517/d287954ds1.htm.

2. Ibid.

3. Ibid.

4. Ibid.

5. Mark Zuckerberg, "Building Global Community," Facebook, February 16, 2017, https://www.facebook.com/notes/mark-zuckerberg/building-global-community/10154544292806634/.

6. Jaron Lanier, *Who Owns the Future?* (New York: Simon & Schuster, 2013), 65.

7. Fred Vogelstein, "The Wired Interview: Facebook's Mark Zuckerberg," *Wired*, June 29, 2009, https://www.wired.com/2009/06/mark-zuckerberg-speaks/.

8. Clive de Freitas, "The Meaning of Search: How It Shapes Our Lives and Builds Brands," Think with Google, October 2013, https://www.thinkwithgoogle.com/marketing-resources/meaning-of-search/.

9. Lanier, *Who Owns the Future?*, 60.

10. Aaron Smith, "Nearly Half of American Adults Are Smartphone Owners," Pew Research Center, March 1, 2012, https://www.pewresearch.org/internet/2012/03/01/nearly-half-of-american-adults-are-smartphone-owners/.

11. "Mobile Fact Sheet," Pew Research Center, June 12, 2019, https://www.pewresearch.org/internet/fact-sheet/mobile/.

12. Andrew Perrin and Madhu Kumar, "About Three-in-Ten U.S. Adults Say They Are 'Almost Constantly' Online," Pew Research Center, July 25, 2019, https://www.pewresearch.org/fact-tank/2019/07/25/americans-going-online-almost-constantly/.

13. See Shoshana Zuboff, *The Age of Surveillance Capitalism: The Fight for a Human Future at the New Frontier of Power* (New York: Public Affairs, 2019), 64–65; Hal R. Varian, curriculum vitae, https://people.ischool.berkeley.edu/~hal/people/hal/vitae.pdf.

14. Zuboff, *The Age of Surveillance Capitalism*, 64–65.

15. Hal R. Varian, "Computer Mediated Transactions," *American Economic Review* 100, no. 2 (2010): 1–10, https://www.aeaweb.org/articles?id=10.1257/aer.100.2.1, 2.

16. Ibid.

17. Ibid.

18. Ibid., 5.

19. *New Mexico v. Google LLC* (D.N.M. Feb. 20, 2020), 1, https://www.nmag.gov/uploads/PressRelease/48737699ae174b30ac51a7eb286e661f/AG_Balderas_Sues_Google_for_Illegally_Collecting_Personal_Data_of_New_Mexican_School_Children.pdf.

20. Cheri Kiesecker, "What's Stored in Your School Google Drive Account? You Might Be Surprised," Missouri Education Watchdog, August 2, 2018, https://web.archive.org/web/20200721185540/http://missourieducationwatchdog.com/whats-stored-in-your-school-google-drive-account-you-might-be-surprised/. See also Claudette Riley, "SPS Says Cybersecurity Allegations Part of a 'Misinformation Campaign,'" *Springfield News-Leader*, February 8, 2019.

21. *New Mexico v. Google LLC*, 12–15.

22. Ibid.

23. Kiesecker, "What's Stored in Your School Google Drive Account?"

24. *New Mexico v. Google LLC*, 12–14.

25. Riley, "SPS Says Cybersecurity Allegations Part of a 'Misinformation Campaign'"; Cheri Kiesecker, "Kids Are Being Bombarded with Online Ads (Sometimes Graphic)—in School. Time to Stop Online Ads to Students?" Missouri Education Watchdog, December 8, 2018, https://web.archive.org/web/20201101142620/https://missourieducationwatchdog.com/kids-are-being-bombarded-with-online-ads-sometimes-graphic-in-school-time-to-stop-online-ads-to-students/.

26. See *New Mexico v. Google LLC*, 12–16; Kiesecker, "Kids Are Being Bombarded with Online Ads."

27. *New Mexico v. Google LLC*, 12.
28. Sarah E. Needleman, "Judge Dismisses New Mexico Lawsuit against Google over Children's Data Privacy," *Wall Street Journal*, September 29, 2020, https://www.wsj.com/articles/judge-dismisses-new-mexico-lawsuit-against-google-over-childrens-data-privacy-11601392392.
29. Varian, "Computer Mediated Transactions," 5.
30. Freitas, "The Meaning of Search."
31. Lanier, *Who Owns the Future?*, 60.
32. Sergey Brin and Lawrence Page, "The Anatomy of a Large-Scale Hypertextual Web Search Engine," *Computer Networks and ISDN Systems* 30 (1998), Appendix A, https://storage.googleapis.com/pub-tools-public-publication-data/pdf/334.pdf.
33. Zuboff, *The Age of Surveillance Capitalism*, 67–92.
34. Ibid., 64–97.
35. Nick Statt, "Google Will Stop Scanning Your Gmail Messages to Sell Targeted Ads," The Verge, June 23, 2017, https://www.theverge.com/2017/6/23/15862492/google-gmail-advertising-targeting-privacy-cloud-business.
36. Stefanie Olsen, "Facebook's Sandberg: Growth before Monetization," CNET, July 22, 2008, https://www.cnet.com/news/facebooks-sandberg-growth-before-monetization/.
37. Ibid.
38. Tristan Harris, "How Technology Is Hijacking Your Mind—from a Magician and Google Design Ethicist," Medium, May 18, 2016, https://medium.com/thrive-global/how-technology-hijacks-peoples-minds-from-a-magician-and-google-s-design-ethicist-56d62ef5edf3.
39. Ibid.
40. Ibid.
41. Ibid.
42. Robinson Meyer, "Everything We Know about Facebook's Secret Mood Manipulation Experiment," *The Atlantic*, June 28, 2014, https://www.theatlantic.com/technology/archive/2014/06/everything-we-know-about-facebooks-secret-mood-manipulation-experiment/373648/.
43. Harris, "How Technology is Hijacking Your Mind."
44. Ibid.
45. Nicholas Carlson, "Facebook Just Made a Major Change to What Users See on the Site," Business Insider, August 6, 2013, https://www.businessinsider.com/

facebook-just-changed-the-kinds-of-stories-youll-see-when-you-re-load-your-news-feed-2013-8.

46. See Form 10-K for Facebook, Inc. filed with the Securities and Exchange Commission on January 29, 2020, http://d18rnop25nwr6d.cloudfront.net/CIK-0001326801/45290cc0-656d-4a88-a2f3-147c8de86506.pdf, and Form 10-K for Alphabet Inc. filed with the Securities and Exchange Commission on February 3, 2020, https://www.sec.gov/Archives/edgar/data/1652044/000165204420000008/goog10-k2019.htm.

47. Venkatesh Rao, "The Premium Mediocre Life of Maya Millennial," Ribbonfarm, August 17, 2017, https://www.ribbonfarm.com/2017/08/17/the-premium-mediocre-life-of-maya-millennial/.

48. Eric Berger, "American Kids Would Much Rather be YouTubers Than Astronauts," ArsTechnica, July 16, 2019, https://arstechnica.com/science/2019/07/american-kids-would-much-rather-be-youtubers-than-astronauts/.

49. Lanier, *Who Owns the Future?*, 56–57.

50. Joseph Cox, "I Gave a Bounty Hunter $300. Then He Located Our Phone," Vice, January 8, 2019, https://www.vice.com/en/article/nepxbz/i-gave-a-bounty-hunter-300-dollars-located-phone-microbilt-zumigo-tmobile.

51. Dorian Lynskey, "'Alexa, Are You Invading My Privacy?'—The Dark Side of Our Voice Assistants," *The Guardian*, October 9, 2019, https://www.theguardian.com/technology/2019/oct/09/alexa-are-you-invading-my-privacy-the-dark-side-of-our-voice-assistants.

CHAPTER 6: ANTI-SOCIAL MEDIA

1. "UK Smartphone Usage Data 2014," Tecmark, https://www.tecmark.co.uk/resources/insights/uk-smartphone-usage-data-2014.

2. Tony Reinke, *12 Ways Your Phone Is Changing You* (Wheaton, Illinois: Crossway, 2017), 16.

3. Adrian F. Ward, Kristen Duke, Ayelet Gneezy, and Maarten W. Bos, "Brain Drain: The Mere Presence of One's Own Smartphone Reduces Available Cognitive Capacity," *Journal of the Association of Consumer Research* 2, no. 2 (2017): 140–154, http://dx.doi.org/10.1086/691462, 149.

4. Robinson Meyer, "Your Smartphone Reduces Your Brainpower, Even If It's Just Sitting There," *The Atlantic*, August 2, 2017.

5. L. D. Rosen, Mark Carrier, and N.A. Cheever, "Facebook and Texting Made Me Do It: Media-Induced Task-Switching while Studying," *Computers in Human Behavior* 29, no. 3 (2013): 948–58.

6. Jean Twenge, "Have Smartphones Destroyed a Generation?" *The Atlantic*, September 2017.

7. Ibid.

8. Ibid.

9. Kaitlyn Burnell et al., "Passive Social Networking Site Use and Well-Being: The Mediating Roles of Social Comparison and the Fear of Missing Out," *Journal of Psychological Research on Cyberspace* 13, no. 3, Article 5 (2019), https://cyberpsychology.eu/article/view/12271/10710.

10. Przybylski, Murayama, DeHaan, and Gladwell, "Motivational, Emotional, and Behavioral Correlates of Fear of Missing Out," *Computers in Human Behavior* 29, no. 4 (2013), 1841–48, https://doi.org.10.1016/j.chb.2013.02.014.

11. "FoMO" has consistently been found to be related to greater levels of social media use [Z. G. Baker, H. Krieger, and A. S. LeRoy, "Fear of Missing Out: Relationships with Depression, Mindfulness, and Physical Symptoms," *Translational Issues in Psychological Science* 2, no. 3 (2016): 275–82, https://doi.org/10.1037/tps0000075]; David Blackwell et al., "Extraversion, Neuroticism, Attachment Style and Fear of Missing Out as Predictors of Social Media Use and Addiction," *Personality and Individual Differences* 116 (2017): 69–72.

12. See Table 2 in Jean M. Twenge, Brian H. Spitzberg, and W. Keith Campbell, "Less In-Person Social Interaction with Peers among U.S. Adolescents in the 21st Century and Links to Loneliness," *Journal of Social and Personal Relationships* 36, no. 6 (2019): 1892–1913, https://doi.org/10.1177/0265407519836170.

13. Ibid., Table 1.

14. "Center for Collegiate Mental Health 2019 Annual Report," Center for Collegiate Mental Health at Penn State University, January 2020, https://ccmh.psu.edu/assets/docs/2019-CCMH-Annual-Report_3.17.20.pdf.

15. Twenge, "Have Smartphones Destroyed a Generation?"

16. Ibid.

17. Ibid. For a broader review of the available literature, see J. Haidt and J. Twenge, *Social Media Use and Mental Health: A Review*, unpublished manuscript, New York University, 2019, https://docs.google.com/document/d/1w-HOfseF2wF9YIpXwUUtP65-olnkPyWcgF5BiAtBEyo/mobilebasic#h.xi8mrj7rpf37.

18. Haidt and Twenge, *Social Media Use and Mental Health*.

19. For recent increase after years of stability, see Brianna Abbott, "Youth Suicide Rate Increased 56% in Decade, CDC Says," *Wall Street Journal*,

October 17, 2019, https://www.wsj.com/articles/youth-suicide-rate-rises-56-in-decade-cdc-says-11571284861. For 1990s decline, see K. M. Lubell, S. R. Kegler, A. E. Crosby, and D. Karch, "Suicide Trends among Youths and Young Adults Aged 10–24 Years—United States, 1990–2004," National Center for Injury Prevention and Control, Centers for Disease Control, September 7, 2007, https://www.cdc.gov/mmwr/preview/mmwrhtml/mm5635a2.htm.

20. Abbott, "Youth Suicide Rate Increased 56% in Decade."
21. Twenge, "Have Smartphones Destroyed a Generation?"
22. Louise Matsakis, "How Pro-Eating Disorder Posts Evade Filters on Social Media," *Wired*, June 13, 2018, https://www.wired.com/story/how-pro-eating-disorder-posts-evade-social-media-filters/.
23. Hannah Seligson, "The New Unsexy Sexy Marketplace," *New York Times*, September 26, 2020, https://www.nytimes.com/topic/subject/sex.
24. Ashley Carman, "OnlyFans Stars Say TikTok Is Making Them Rich," The Verge, September 17, 2020, https://www.theverge.com/2020/9/17/21439657/onlyfans-tiktok-subscribers-videos-fans.
25. Jerold J. Block, "Issues for DSM-V: Internet Addiction," *American Journal of Psychiatry* 163, no. 3 (March 2008): 306–7, https://ajp.psychiatryonline.org/doi/pdf/10.1176/appi.ajp.2007.07101556.
26. Rachel Moss, "This Is What It's Like to Be Targeted by Baby Ads after Miscarriage or IVF Struggles," HuffPost, September 29, 2019, https://www.huffingtonpost.co.uk/entry/women-affected-by-miscarriage-and-infertility-are-being-targeted-with-baby-ads-on-facebook_uk_5d7f7c42e4b00d69059bd88a.
27. William J. Brady et al., "Emotion Shapes the Diffusion of Moralized Content in Social Networks," *Proceedings of the National Academy of Sciences* 114, no. 28 (2017): 7313–18, https://vanbavellab.hosting.nyu.edu/documents/Brady.etal.2017.PNAS.pdf.
28. "Partisan Conflict and Congressional Outreach," Pew Research Center, February 23, 2017, https://www.pewresearch.org/politics/2017/02/23/partisan-conflict-and-congressional-outreach/.
29. Kevin Roose, "The Making of a YouTube Radical," *New York Times*, June 8, 2019.
30. Ibid.
31. Ibid.
32. Ibid.
33. Ibid.

34. Max Fisher and Amanda Taub, "On YouTube's Digital Playground, an Open Gate for Pedophiles," *New York Times*, June 3, 2019.

35. Ibid.

36. "Sen. Hawley Announces Legislation Forcing YouTube to Stop Catering to Pedophiles," announcement by office of Senator Josh Hawley, June 6, 2019, https://www.hawley.senate.gov/ sen-hawley-announces-legislation-forcing-youtube-stop-catering-pedophiles.

37. Jonathan Haidt and Tobias Rose-Stockwell, "The Dark Psychology of Social Networks," *The Atlantic*, December 2019, https://www.theatlantic.com/ magazine/archive/2019/12/social-media-democracy/600763/.

38. See, for example, Dawn S. Carlson, Ranida B. Harris, and Kenneth J. Harris, "Social Media Reactions: The Implications for Job Performance," *Journal of Psychology* 159, no. 6 (March 2019).

39. Roose, "The Making of a YouTube Radical."

CHAPTER 7: THE CENSORS

1. Emma-Jo Morris and Gabrielle Fonrouge, "Smoking-Gun Email Reveals How Hunter Biden Introduced Ukrainian Businessman to VP Dad," *New York Post*, October 14, 2020.

2. Sarah Frier and Kurt Wagner, "Facebook Slows Spread of N.Y. Post Biden Story to Fact-Check," Bloomberg News, October 14, 2020, https://www. bloomberg.com/news/articles/2020-10-14/ facebook-to-reduce-distribution-of-new-york-post-story-on-bidens.

3. Mike Isaac and Kate Conger, "Twitter Changes Course after Republicans Claim 'Election Interference,'" *New York Times*, October 15, 2020.

4. "Twitter Lifts Freeze from New York Post Account after Policy Reversal," *The Guardian*, October 30, 2020.

5. Isaac and Conger, "Twitter Changes Course."

6. Kevin Johnson, "DNI Ratcliffe: Russia Disinformation Not behind Published Emails Targeting Biden; FBI Reviewing," *USA Today*, October 19, 2020.

7. See Bob Moser, "The Reckoning of Morris Dees and the Southern Poverty Law Center," *New Yorker*, March 21, 2019, https://www.newyorker.com/ news/news-desk/ the-reckoning-of-morris-dees-and-the-southern-poverty-law-center.

8. "Breaking the News: Censorship, Suppression, and the 2020 Election," hearing before the Senate Judiciary Committee, November 17, 2020, Bloomberg Government transcription.

9. Ibid.

10. Ibid. See also Senator Josh Hawley, "Hawley Reveals Big Tech Coordination Tool to Covertly Track, Censor Users across Internet," YouTube, November 17, 2020, https://www.youtube.com/watch?v=79M32z1LgD8&feature=youtu.be.

11. "Breaking the News: Censorship, Suppression, and the 2020 Election," hearing before the Senate Judiciary Committee.

12. Ibid.

13. Ibid.

14. Emily Birnbaum (@birnbaum_e), "Facebook tells me Centra, the tool Hawley called out in his line of questioning, is used to aid investigation into subjects like coordinated inauthentic behavior. And Tasks is an internal coordination tool (Zuckerberg described it as an internal 'to-do list.')," Twitter, November 17, 2020, 2:04 p.m., https://twitter.com/birnbaum_e/status/1328776008141574147.

15. Michael Nunez, "Former Facebook Workers: We Routinely Suppressed Conservative News," Gizmodo, May 9, 2016, https://gizmodo.com/former-facebook-workers-we-routinely-suppressed-conser-1775461006.

16. Ibid.

17. Ibid.

18. Ibid.

19. Michael Nunez, "Want to Know What Facebook Really Thinks of Journalists? Here's What Happened When It Hired Some," Gizmodo, May 3, 2016, https://gizmodo.com/want-to-know-what-facebook-really-thinks-of-journalists-1773916117.

20. Laura Hazard Owen, "Mark Zuckerberg Has Thoughts on the Future of News on Facebook," Nieman Lab, June 30, 2015, https://www.niemanlab.org/2015/06/mark-zuckerberg-has-thoughts-on-the-future-of-news-on-facebook/.

21. Nunez, "Former Facebook Workers."

22. Maxwell Tani, "Top Clinton Ally Hints at a Major Battle against Fake News," Business Insider, December 6, 2016, https://www.businessinsider.com/david-brock-fake-news-2016-12; Callum Borchers, "How Hillary Clinton Might Have Inspired Trump's 'Fake News' Attacks," *Washington Post,* January 3, 2018, https://www.washingtonpost.com/news/the-fix/wp/2018/01/03/how-hillary-clinton-might-have-inspired-trumps-fake-news-attacks/.

23. Ben Smith and Mat Honan, "Facebook Has Begun to Rank News Organizations by Trust, Zuckerberg Says," Buzzfeed News, May 1, 2018,

https://www.buzzfeednews.com/article/bensmith/
facebook-has-begun-to-rank-news-organizations-by-trust.

24. Laura Hazard Owen, "Facebook's Campbell Brown: 'This Is Not about Us
     Trying to Make Everybody Happy,'" Nieman Lab, February 13, 2018,
     https://www.niemanlab.org/2018/02/facebooks-campbell-brown-this-is-not-about-
     us-trying-to-make-everybody-happy/.

25. "Facebook Engagement Trends in March: The Winners and Losers,"
     NewsWhip, April 12, 2018, https://www.newswhip.com/2018/04/
     facebook-engagements-march-2018/.

26. Paris Martineau, "Conservative Publishers Hit Hardest by Facebook News
     Feed Change," The Outline, March 5, 2018, https://theoutline.com/
     post/3599/
     conservative-publishers-hit-hardest-by-facebook-news-feed-
     change?zd=4&zi=6ki6jclk.

27. Chris White, "'Deeply Offensive': Leaked Videos Show Google Leadership
     Reacting to Trump's Victory," Daily Caller, September 13, 2018, https://
     dailycaller.com/2018/09/13/google-trump-election-video-sergey-brin/.

28. Allum Bokhari, "Leaked Video: Google Leadership's Dismayed Reaction to
     Trump Election," Breitbart, September 12, 2018, https://www.breitbart.
     com/tech/2018/09/12/leaked-video-google-leaderships-dismayed-
     reaction-to-trump-election/.

29. For a primer, see David Shultz, "Could Google Influence the Presidential
     Election?" *Science*, October 25, 2016.

30. Robert Epstein and Ronald E. Robertson, "The Search Engine
     Manipulation Effect (SEME) and Its Possible Impact on the Outcome of
     Elections," Proceedings of the National Academy of Sciences USA 112, no.
     33 (August 4, 2015).

31. Robert Epstein, "Why Google Poses a Serious Threat to Democracy, and
     How to End That Threat," testimony before the U.S. Senate Judiciary
     Subcommittee on the Constitution, June 16, 2019, https://www.judiciary.
     senate.gov/imo/media/doc/Epstein%20Testimony.pdf.

32. Ibid.

33. Ibid. See also Robert Epstein and Emily M. Williams, "Evidence of
     Systematic Political Bias in Online Search Results in the Last 10 Days
     Leading Up to the 2018 U.S. Midterm Election," paper presented at the 99th
     annual meeting of the Western Psychological Association, April 2019.

34. Epstein, "Why Google Poses a Serious Threat to Democracy."

35. Ibid. See also Robert Epstein, Roger Mohr Jr., and Jeremy Martinez, "The
     Search Suggestion Effect (SSE): How Search Suggestions Can Be Used to

Shift Opinions and Voting Preferences Dramatically and without People's Awareness," *American Institute for Behavioral Research and Technology*, April 26, 2018, https://aibrt.org/downloads/EPSTEIN_MOHR_%26_MARTINEZ_2018-WPA-The_Search_Suggestion_Effect-SSE-WP-17-03.pdf.

36. Epstein, Mohr, and Martinez, "The Search Suggestion Effect."
37. Ibid.
38. Ibid; see also Epstein and Robertson, "The Search Engine Manipulation Effect."
39. Eric Lieberman, "Google's New Fact-Check Feature Almost Exclusively Targets Conservative Sites," Daily Caller, January 9, 2018, https://dailycaller.com/2018/01/09/googles-new-fact-check-feature-almost-exclusively-targets-conservative-sites/.
40. Eric Lieberman, "Google Suspends Fact Check Project, Crediting the DCNF Investigation with Decision," Daily Caller, January 19, 2018, https://dailycaller.com/2018/01/19/google-ends-fact-check/.
41. Tristan Justice, "A Recap of NBC's Failed Attempt to Deplatform the Federalist on Google," The Federalist, June 22, 220, https://thefederalist.com/2020/06/22/a-recap-of-nbcs-failed-attempt-to-deplatform-the-federalist-on-google/.
42. Jason Bursztynsky, "Vice Media CEO Slams Big Tech as 'Great Threat to Journalism' in Layoffs Memo," CNBC, May 15, 2020, https://www.cnbc.com/2020/05/15/vice-media-ceo-slams-big-tech-as-great-threat-to-journalism.html.
43. Google's US Ad Revenues to Drop for the First Time," Emarketer, June 22, 2020, https://www.emarketer.com/newsroom/index.php/google-ad-revenues-to-drop-for-the-first-time/.
44. "Newspapers Fact Sheet," Pew Research Center, July 9, 2019, https://www.journalism.org/fact-sheet/newspapers/.
45. Bradley Johnson, "Internet Media's Share of U.S. Ad Spending Has More Than Tripled over the Past Decade," *Ad Age*, December 30, 2019, https://adage.com/article/year-end-lists-2019/internet-medias-share-us-ad-spending-has-more-tripled-over-past-decade/2221701.
46. Ibid.
47. Elisa Shearer and Katerina Eva Matsa, "News Use across Social Media Platforms 2018," Pew Research Center, September 10, 2018, https://www.journalism.org/2018/09/10/news-use-across-social-media-platforms-2018/.

48. For an excellent summary of the Google model, see Australian Competition & Consumer Commission, *Digital Platforms Inquiry Final Report*, 209–11.

49. Joanne Lipman, "Tech Overlords Google and Facebook Have Used Monopoly to Rob Journalism of Its Revenue," *USA Today*, June 11, 2019; Australian Competition & Consumer Commission, *Digital Platforms Inquiry Final Report*.

50. Phillip Longman, "Starving the News," *Washington Monthly*, November/December 2020, https://washingtonmonthly.com/magazine/november-december-2020/starving-the-news/.

51. Lipman, "Tech Overlords Google and Facebook Have Used Monopoly to Rob Journalism of Its Revenue"; see also News Media Alliance, *Google Benefit from News Content*, June 2019, http://www.newsmediaalliance.org/wp-content/uploads/2019/06/Google-Benefit-from-News-Content.pdf; Marc Tracy, "Google Made $4.7 Billion from the News Industry in 2018, Study Says," *New York Times,* June 9, 2019, https://www.nytimes.com/2019/06/09/business/media/google-news-industry-antitrust.html.

52. Bursztynsky, "Vice Media CEO Slams Big Tech."

53. Joanne Lipman, "Tech Overlords Google and Facebook Have Used Monopoly to Rob Journalism of Its Revenue."

54. Ibid.

55. See Australian Competition & Consumer Commission, *Digital Platforms Inquiry Final Report*, discussion on AMP, chapter 5.

56. Alexis C. Madrigal and Robinson Meyer, "How Facebook's Chaotic Push into Video Cost Hundreds of Journalists Their Jobs," *The Atlantic*, October 18, 2018.

57. John Herrman, "Territory Annexed," The Awl, January 8, 2015, https://www.theawl.com/2015/01/territory-annexed/.

58. Steve Jobs, interview by Walt Mossberg and Kara Swisher at D8 conference, June 1, 2010.

59. Joshua Benton, "What Apple's New Subscription Policy Means for News: New Rules, New Incentives, New Complaints," Nieman Lab, February 15, 2011, https://www.niemanlab.org/2011/02/what-apples-new-subscription-policy-means-for-news-new-rules-new-incentives-new-complaints/; Megan Garber and Andrew Phelps, "Newsstand, Reader, iCloud: 3 Takeaways for the News Business from Today's Apple Announcement," Nieman Lab, June 6, 2011, https://www.niemanlab.org/2011/06/newsstand-reader-icloud-3-takeaways-for-the-news-business-from-todays-apple-announcement/.

60. Rob Pegoraro, "Apple Is Trying to Be the Future of News. Again," *Washington Post*, March 25, 2019, https://www.washingtonpost.com/outlook/2019/03/25/apple-is-trying-be-future-news-again/.

CHAPTER 8: NEW WORLD ORDER

1. George H. W. Bush, "October 1, 1990: Address to the United Nations," Miller Center, https://millercenter.org/the-presidency/presidential-speeches/october-1-1990-address-united-nations.
2. Ibid.
3. Ibid.
4. In a 2016 study by enterprise intelligence firm Craft of S&P 500 market capitalization per employee, Apple, Facebook, and Alphabet all made the top fifty. Facebook was number three on the list, which was dominated by firms whose business models depend largely on extractive profits, from energy firms to pharmaceutical monopolists. "S&P 500—Market Value Per Employee Perspective," Craft, https://craft.co/reports/s-p-500-market-value-per-employee-perspective. See also Jon Hilsenrath and Bob Davis, "America's Dazzling Tech Boom Has a Downside: Not Enough Jobs," *Wall Street Journal*, October 12, 2016, https://www.wsj.com/articles/americas-dazzling-tech-boom-has-a-downside-not-enough-jobs-1476282355.
5. For an illustration of the digital platforms' asset hoarding relative to investment, see net lending positions for Google, Apple, and Facebook on page 18 of Senator Marco Rubio, "American Investment in the 21st Century," May 15, 2019, https://www.rubio.senate.gov/public/_cache/files/9f25139a-6039-465a-9cf1-feb5567aebb7/4526E9620A9A7DB74267AB EA5881022F.5.15.2019.-final-project-report-american-investment.pdf.
6. Jaron Lanier, *Who Owns the Future?* (New York: Simon & Schuster, 2013), 2.
7. In a survey of IT leaders and infrastructure managers, cloud firm INAP found that 81 percent predict that by 2025, most data center and network tasks will be fully automated. Ryan Hunt, "IT Pros Predict What Infrastructure and Data Centers Will Look Like by 2025," INAP, February 27, 2020, https://www.inap.com/blog/data-center-cloud-predictions-2025/.
8. "The Silicon Six and Their $100 Billion Global Tax Gap," Fair Tax Mark, December 2019, https://fairtaxmark.net/wp-content/uploads/2019/12/Silicon-Six-Report-5-12-19.pdf.
9. Rubio, "American Investment in the 21st Century," 18.
10. Pat Garofalo, Matt Stoller, and Olivia Webb, "Understanding Amazon: Making the 21st-Century Gatekeeper Safe for Democracy," American

Economic Liberties Project, July 2020, https://www.economicliberties.us/wp-content/uploads/2020/07/Working-Paper-Series-on-Corporate-Power_5-FINAL.pdf.

11. Original white paper preserved by the internet archive at "Libra White Paper," Libra Association, https://web.archive.org/web/20190701172919if_/https://libra.org/en-US/white-paper/. Version 2.0 is available at "Libra White Paper," Libra Association, April 2020, https://libra.org/en-US/white-paper/#cover-letter.

12. Lawrence Mishel, Elise Gould, and Josh Bivens, "Wage Stagnation in Nine Charts," Economic Policy Institute, January 6, 2015, https://www.epi.org/publication/charting-wage-stagnation/.

13. Robert E. Scott and Zane Mokhiber, "Growing China Trade Deficit Cost 3.7 Million American Jobs between 2001 and 2018," Economic Policy Institute, January 30, 2020, https://www.epi.org/publication/growing-china-trade-deficits-costs-us-jobs/.

14. Robert McMillan and Tripp Mickle, "Apple to Start Putting Sensitive Encryption Keys in China," *Wall Street Journal*, February 24, 2018, https://www.wsj.com/articles/apple-to-start-putting-sensitive-encryption-keys-in-china-1519497574.

15. Daniel Van Boom, "China's State-Owned Telecom Company Is Now Storing iCloud Data," CNET, July 18, 2018, https://www.cnet.com/news/chinas-state-owned-telecom-company-is-now-storing-icloud-data/.

16. Vicki Xiuzhong Xu et al., "Uyghurs for Sale," Australian Strategic Policy Institute, March 1, 2020, https://www.aspi.org.au/report/uyghurs-sale.

17. Reed Albergotti, "Apple Is Lobbying against a Bill Aimed at Stopping Forced Labor in China," *Washington Post*, November 20, 2020, https://www.washingtonpost.com/technology/2020/11/20/apple-uighur/.

18. Matt Sheehan, "How Google Took on China—and Lost," *MIT Technology Review*, December 19, 2018, https://www.technologyreview.com/2018/12/19/138307/how-google-took-on-china-and-lost/.

19. Mike Isaac, "Facebook Said to Create Censorship Tool to Get Back into China," *New York Times*, November 22, 2016, https://www.nytimes.com/2016/11/22/technology/facebook-censorship-tool-china.html.

20. Yunan Zhang and Juro Osawa, "Bytedance in Talks to Raise $1.45 Billion for Startup Shopping Spree," The Information, December 6, 2018, https://www.theinformation.com/articles/bytedance-in-talks-to-raise-1-45-billion-for-startup-shopping-spree.

21. Brody Mullins, Rolfe Winkler, and Brent Kendall, "Inside the U.S. Antitrust Probe of Google," *Wall Street Journal*, March 19, 2015, https://www.wsj.com/articles/inside-the-u-s-antitrust-probe-of-google-1426793274.

22. See page 130, note 136, in leaked excerpts from FTC staff memo published by *Wall Street Journal*, August 8, 2012, http://graphics.wsj.com/google-ftc-report/img/ftc-ocr-watermark.pdf.

23. Michael Luca, Tim Wu, Sebastian Couvidat, and Daniel Frank, "Does Google Content Degrade Google Search? Experimental Evidence," Harvard Business School NOM Unit Working Paper No. 16-035, 2015, https://scholarship.law.columbia.edu/cgi/viewcontent.cgi?article=2932&context=faculty_scholarship.

24. "Antitrust: Commission Fines Google €2.42 Billion for Abusing Dominance as Search Engine by Giving Illegal Advantage to Own Comparison Shopping Service," European Commission, June 27, 2017, https://ec.europa.eu/commission/presscorner/detail/en/IP_17_1784.

25. Ibid.

26. "Antitrust: Commission Fines Google €4.34 Billion for Illegal Practices Regarding Android Mobile Devices to Strengthen Dominance of Google's Search Engine," European Commission, July 18, 2018, https://ec.europa.eu/commission/presscorner/detail/en/IP_18_4581.

27. See Figure 2, "Online Platforms and Digital Advertising: Market Study Final Report," UK Competition and Markets Authority, July 1, 2020, 30, https://assets.publishing.service.gov.uk/media/5efc57ed3a6f4023d242ed56/Final_report_1_July_2020_.pdf.

28. Ibid., Appendix M, note 550, https://assets.publishing.service.gov.uk/media/5efb22add3bf7f769c84e016/Appendix_M_-_intermediation_in_open_display_advertising.pdf.

29. Ibid. See also notes 410 and 423.

30. "Antitrust: Commission Fines Google €1.49 Billion for Abusive Practices in Online Advertising," European Commission, March 20, 2019, https://ec.europa.eu/commission/presscorner/detail/en/IP_19_1770.

31. "Justice Department Sues Monopolist Google for Violating Antitrust Laws," Department of Justice, October 20, 2020, https://www.justice.gov/opa/pr/justice-department-sues-monopolist-google-violating-antitrust-laws.

32. Dina Srinivasan, "The Antitrust Case against Facebook: A Monopolist's Journey towards Pervasive Surveillance in Spite of Consumers' Preference for Privacy," *Berkeley Business Law Journal* 16, no. 1 (2019): 39–101, 48, https://lawcat.berkeley.edu/record/1128876?ln=en. See Julie Rawe, "How Safe Is MySpace?" *Time*, June 26, 2006, http://content.time.com/time/

magazine/article/0,9171,1207808,00.html; Susanna Schrobsdorff, "Predator's Playground," *Newsweek*, January 26, 2006, http://www. newsweek.com/predators-playground- 108471; Catherine Dwyer, Starr Hiltz, and Katia Passerini, "Trust and Privacy Concern within Social Networking Sites: A Comparison of Facebook and MySpace," Americas Conference on Information Systems (2007), https://www.researchgate.net/publication/220889809_Trust_and_Privacy_Concern_Within_Social_Networking_Sites_A_Comparison_of_Facebook_and_MySpace.

33. "Facebook Settles FTC Charges That It Deceived Consumers by Failing to Keep Privacy Promises," Federal Trade Commission, November 29, 2011, https://www.ftc.gov/news-events/press-releases/2011/11/facebook-settles-ftc-charges-it-deceived-consumers-failing-keep.

34. "FTC Imposes $5 Billion Penalty and Sweeping New Privacy Restrictions on Facebook," Federal Trade Commission, July 24, 2019, https://www.ftc.gov/news-events/press-releases/2019/07/ftc-imposes-5-billion-penalty-sweeping-new-privacy-restrictions.

35. Casey Newton and Nilay Patel, "'Instagram Can Hurt Us': Mark Zuckerberg Emails Outline Plan to Neutralize Competitors," The Verge, July 29, 2020, https://www.theverge.com/2020/7/29/21345723/facebook-instagram-documents-emails-mark-zuckerberg-kevin-systrom-hearing.

36. Brent Kendall, John D. McKinnon, and Deepa Seetharaman, "FTC Antitrust Probe of Facebook Scrutinizes Its Acquisitions," *Wall Street Journal*, August 1, 2019, https://www.wsj.com/articles/ftc-antitrust-probe-of-facebook-scrutinizes-its-acquisitions-11564683965.

37. Dieter Bohn, "Why Amazon Got Out of the Apple App Store Tax, and Why Other Developers Won't," The Verge, April 3, 2020, https://www.theverge.com/2020/4/3/21206400/apple-tax-amazon-tv-prime-30-percent-developers.

38. See Australian Competition & Consumer Commission, *Digital Platforms Inquiry: Final Report*, June 2019, 223–24.

39. Daniel Ek, "Consumers and Innovators Win on a Level Playing Field," Spotify Newsroom, March 13, 2019, https://newsroom.spotify.com/2019-03-13/consumers-and-innovators-win-on-a-level-playing-field/.

40. Tripp Mickle, "Apple Dominates App Store Search Results, Thwarting Competitors," *Wall Street Journal*, July 23, 2019.

41. "Antitrust: Commission Opens Investigations into Apple's App Store Rules," European Commission, June 16, 2020, https://ec.europa.eu/commission/presscorner/detail/en/ip_20_1073.

42. Petition to FTC by the International Brotherhood of Teamsters, Communications Workers of America, United Food & Commercial

Workers International Union, Service Employees International Union, and Change to Win, February 27, 2020, http://www.changetowin.org/wp-content/uploads/2020/02/Petition-for-Investigation-of-Amazon.pdf.

43. Ibid.

44. Will Oremus, "The Time Jeff Bezos Went Thermonuclear on Diapers.com," *Slate*, October 10, 2013, https://slate.com/technology/2013/10/amazon-book-how-jeff-bezos-went-thermonuclear-on-diapers-com.html.

45. Daisuke Wakabayashi, "Prime Leverage: How Amazon Wields Power in the Technology World," *New York Times*, December 15, 2019, https://www.nytimes.com/2019/12/15/technology/amazon-aws-cloud-competition.html.

46. See, e.g., David Streitfeld, "Writers Feel an Amazon-Hachette Spat," *New York Times*, May 9, 2014.

47. Khadeeja Safdar and Dana Mattioli, "Nike to Stop Selling Directly to Amazon," *Wall Street Journal*, November 13, 2019, https://www.wsj.com/articles/nike-to-stop-selling-directly-to-amazon-11573615633.

48. Matt Day and Spencer Soper, "Amazon U.S. Online Market Share Estimate Cut to 38% from 47%," Bloomberg, June 13, 2019, https://www.bloomberg.com/news/articles/2019-06-13/emarketer-cuts-estimate-of-amazon-s-u-s-online-market-share.

49. Mark Zuckerberg, "Building Global Community," Facebook, February 16, 2017, https://www.facebook.com/notes/mark-zuckerberg/building-global-community/10154544292806634/.

CHAPTER 9: RIGGING WASHINGTON

1. Remarks from Senator James Exon reported in the *Congressional Record* 141, no. 94 (June 9, 1995), https://www.congress.gov/congressional-record/1995/06/09/senate-section/article/S8087-4.

2. *Stratton Oakmont, Inc v. Prodigy Services Co.*, 1995 WL 323710, *3 (Supreme Court NY, May 24, 1995).

3. *Reno v. ACLU*, 521 U.S. 844.

4. See 47 U.S.C. Section 230(f)(3).

5. See *Zeran v. America Online, Inc.*, 129 F.3d 327, 330, 332 (4th Circuit, 1997); *Batzel v. Smith*, 333 F.3d 1018, 1031, and n.18 (9th Circuit, 2003).

6. See Section 230(c)(2)(A).

7. See *Barnes v. Yahoo!, Inc.*, 570 F.3d 1096, 1105 (9th Circuit, 2009); *e-ventures Worldwide, LLC v. Google, Inc.*, 2017 WL 2210029, *3 (MD Fla., February 8, 2017).

8.   *Zeran v. America Online, Inc.* For recent Supreme Court analysis of these issues, see statement of Justice Thomas respecting the denial of certiorari, *Malwarebytes, Inc. v. Enigma Software Group USA, LLC.*

9.   See linked list, "Google-Funded Groups," in "Google's Chorus of (Paid) Supporters," Tech Transparency Project, Campaign for Accountability, October 29, 2019, https://www.techtransparencyproject.org/articles/googles-chorus-supporters.

10. Kenneth P. Vogel, "Google Critic Ousted from Think Tank Funded by the Tech Giant," *New York Times*, August 30, 2017.

11. Ibid.

12. "Our Story," New America Foundation, https://www.newamerica.org/our-story/.

13. Vogel, "Google Critic Ousted from Think Tank Funded by the Tech Giant."

14. "Our Funding," New America Foundation, https://www.newamerica.org/our-funding/donate/.

15. Vogel, "Google Critic Ousted from Think Tank Funded by the Tech Giant."

16. Data from Open Secrets.

17. Brody Mullins and Jack Nicas, "Paying Professors: Inside Google's Academic Influence Campaign," *Wall Street Journal*, July 14, 2017, https://www.wsj.com/articles/paying-professors-inside-googles-academic-influence-campaign-1499785286.

18. Ibid.

19. Daisuke Wakabayashi, "Big Tech Funds a Think Tank Pushing for Fewer Rules. For Big Tech," *New York Times*, July 24, 2020, https://www.nytimes.com/2020/07/24/technology/global-antitrust-institute-google-amazon-qualcomm.html.

20. "A Whopping 75% of FTC Officials Have Revolving Door Conflicts with Tech Corporations and Other Industries," Public Citizen, May 23, 2019, https://www.citizen.org/news/a-whopping-75-of-ftc-officials-have-revolving-door-conflicts-with-tech-corporations-and-other-industries/.

21. Brody Mullins, Rolfe Winkler, and Brent Kendall, "Inside the U.S. Antitrust Probe of Google," *Wall Street Journal*, March 19, 2015.

22. Ibid.

23. Brody Mullins, "Google Makes Most of Close Ties to the White House," *Wall Street Journal*, March 24, 2015, https://www.wsj.com/articles/google-makes-most-of-close-ties-to-white-house-1427242076.

24. Mullins et al., "Inside the U.S. Antitrust Probe of Google."

25. Ibid.

26. Ibid.

CHAPTER 10: WHAT EACH OF US CAN DO

1. Abraham Kuyper, *Christianity and the Class Struggle*, trans. Dirk Jellema (Grand Rapids, Michigan: Piet Hein Publishers, 1950) 48, n.33.
2. For example, see Brandon McGinley, "Living Liturgically," Church Life Journal, December 4, 2020, https://churchlifejournal.nd.edu/articles/living-liturgically/.
3. Allison Aubrey, "A Family Finds a Way to Wean Themselves from Electronic Devices," NPR, February 12, 2018, https://www.npr.org/2018/02/12/585032297/1-family-finds-a-way-to-wean-themselves-from-electronic-devices.

CHAPTER 11: A NEW POLITICS

1. David Ramsay, *The History of the American Revolution*, volume 1 (Philadelphia: 1798), 32–33.
2. Benjamin Franklin, *Information to Those Who Would Remove to America*, March 1783 pamphlet, quoted in Carl Van Doren, *Benjamin Franklin* (New York: Viking Press, 1938), 704.
3. See James L. Huston, "The American Revolutionaries, the Political Economy of Aristocracy, and the American Concept of the Distribution of Wealth, 1765–1900," American Historical Review (October 1993), 1083–84.
4. Alexis de Tocqueville, *Democracy in America* (New York: Mentor, 1956), 26.
5. See Martin J. Sklar, *The Corporate Reconstruction of American Capitalism*, 93–117.
6. "Antitrust: Commission Fines Google €2.42 Billion for Abusing Dominance as Search Engine by Giving Illegal Advantage to Own Comparison Shopping Service," European Commission, June 27, 2017, https://ec.europa.eu/commission/presscorner/detail/en/IP_17_1784.
7. See Figure 2, "Online Platforms and Digital Advertising: Market Study Final Report," UK Competition and Markets Authority, July 1, 2020, 30, https://assets.publishing.service.gov.uk/media/5efc57ed3a6f4023d242ed56/Final_report_1_July_2020_.pdf.
8. *United States v. Microsoft Corp.*, 253 F.3d 34 (D.C. Cir. 2001).
9. "Online Platforms and Digital Advertising," UK Competition and Markets Authority.
10. Dina Srinivasan, "The Antitrust Case against Facebook" 84. See also Social Media Fact Sheet, Pew Research Center, February 5, 2018, (69% of U.S. adults use social media; 68% of U.S. adults use Facebook).
11. Srinivasan, "The Antitrust Case against Facebook," 83.
12. Ibid., 46–53.

13. Ibid.
14. Ibid., 97.
15. Ibid., 70.
16. Ibid.
17. Ibid. See also *ACSI E-Business Report 2018*, American Customer Satisfaction Index, July 24, 2018, https://www.theacsi.org/news-and-resources/customer-satisfaction-reports/report-archive/acsi-e-business-report-2018.
18. Srinivasan, "The Antitrust Case against Facebook," 98–99.
19. Michael Lind, "The Tech Monsters," Tablet, August 31, 2020, https://www.tabletmag.com/sections/news/articles/the-tech-monsters.
20. Ibid.
21. Ibid.
22. See Jonathan Haidt, "More Social Media Regulation," *Politico*, https://www.politico.com/interactives/2019/how-to-fix-politics-in-america/polarization/more-social-media-regulation/. See also Haidt and Twenge, *Social Media Use and Mental Health: A Review*.
23. Chris Hughes, "It's Time to Break Up Facebook," *New York Times*, May 9, 2019.
24. "President Demands Railroad Control," *New York Times*, October 20, 1905.
25. Theodore Roosevelt, *An Autobiography* (New York: Da Capo Press, 1985), 439.

INDEX

189

194   *Index*